D1035523

WITHDRAWN

CONFIDENTIAL
SECRETARY

ALSO BY ROBERT J. DONOVAN

The Assassins
Eisenhower: The Inside Story
My First Fifty Years in Politics (with Joseph W. Martin, Jr.)
PT 109: *John F. Kennedy in World War II*
The Future of the Republican Party
Conflict and Crisis: The Presidency of Harry S Truman, 1945–1948
Tumultuous Years: The Presidency of Harry S Truman, 1949–1953
Nemesis: Truman and Johnson in the Coils of War in Asia
The Second Victory: The Marshall Plan and the Postwar Revival of Europe

926
W591d

CONFIDENTIAL
SECRETARY

ANN WHITMAN'S 20 YEARS WITH EISENHOWER AND ROCKEFELLER

ROBERT J. DONOVAN

E. P. DUTTON  NEW YORK

Copyright © 1988 by Robert J. Donovan
All rights reserved. Printed in the U.S.A.

No part of this publication may be reproduced or transmitted
in any form or by any means, electronic or mechanical, including
photocopy, recording, or any information storage and retrieval
system now known or to be invented, without permission in writing
from the publisher, except by a reviewer who wishes to quote
brief passages in connection with a review written for inclusion
in a magazine, newspaper, or broadcast.

Published in the United States by E. P. Dutton,
a division of NAL Penguin Inc.,
2 Park Avenue, New York, N.Y. 10016.

Published simultaneously in Canada
by Fitzhenry and Whiteside, Limited, Toronto.

Library of Congress Cataloging-in-Publication Data

Donovan, Robert J.
Confidential secretary : Ann Whitman's 20 years with Eisenhower
and Rockefeller / Robert J. Donovan. —1st ed.
p.   cm.
Bibliography: p.
Includes index.
ISBN 0-525-24644-4
1.   United States—Politics and government—1953–1961.
2. United States—Politics and government—1974–1977.
3. Whitman, Ann, 1908–.
4. Eisenhower, Dwight D. (Dwight David), 1890–1969.
5. Rockefeller, Nelson A. (Nelson Aldrich), 1908–1979.
6. Private secretaries—United States—Biography.   I. Title.
E835.D598   1988
973.92—dc 19   87-36416
CIP

Designed by REM Studio

1   3   5   7   9   10   8   6   4   2

First Edition

Eight pages of illustrations follow page 80.

To two great editors and great friends of mine,
Evan W. Thomas
and
Nick B. Williams

GA Γ Jun5 '89

2-22-89 Coutts 18.95

88-6651

The world's finest secretary!
—DWIGHT D. EISENHOWER

PREFACE

Ann Whitman, a bright, cosmopolitan, and energetic woman, held the highly demanding job as confidential secretary and assistant to President Dwight D. Eisenhower throughout his two terms. Then for ten years she was confidential secretary and executive assistant to Governor Nelson A. Rockefeller of New York. After that she was chief of staff and confidential secretary to Vice-President Rockefeller in the Ford administration—the first woman ever to hold the position of chief of staff. If Rockefeller had realized his highest ambition in 1960 or 1964, Mrs. Whitman doubtless would have been back in the White House again as confidential secretary to another president.

The life of a confidential secretary to a president is one that few outsiders can glimpse because of the intimate nature of the work involved and the subtle, indefinable, close relationship between the two. In the years between 1953 and 1961, when she was with President Eisenhower, it might have been supposed that Ann Whitman had a staid job in a staid administration. The truth is quite the opposite. The number and variety of emergencies and crises that filled her life in those eight years are astonishing. For her the job meant fun, drama, adventure, misadventure, and misery in endless combinations. From one to another she struggled through situations that were alternately grave, comical, novel, frantic, delicate, infuriating, elating, and exhausting. Some of the wonderfully preposterous things that happened to her are completely out of character with the image of a sedate secretary taking dictation from a serious general-turned-president. Because Eisenhower traveled extensively around the world, Ann's friends used to say that no other secretary had ever slept in so many castles and palaces as she. Indeed the story of her career counteracts a recent trend toward belittling the title of secretary. Mrs. Whitman's importance to Eisenhower transcended her title. He placed great trust in her, gave her wide responsibilities, and had a warm affection for her.

After having worked for ten years for him—eight in Washington and two during his retirement—Ann moved on to the less exalting but nevertheless stimulating, often opulent, and sometimes quirky environment surrounding Governor Rockefeller. When she flew from New York to Albany with him in January 1965, the importance of her role was felt around the capitol immediately. She took over much of his correspondence. She became the doorkeeper to his office, a confidante, an adviser, a person to stay on the right side of, in the opinion of many of her colleagues. Most of them were fond of her, but as also had been the case in the White House, some others feared her, at least at times. Still others believe to this day that her good advice saved their careers.

In the debris of Watergate, Ann returned to Washington in 1974 with Vice-President Rockefeller and found herself in her most difficult role. After years of speaking frankly to him, she now felt obliged on the basis of her own experience in the White House to tell him not once, but time and again, that he could not do certain things he wanted to do because he was vice-president, not president. It all became a little tiresome for Rockefeller and seemingly played a part in bringing about a turning point in

Ann's life. Events proved the correctness of her advice to him.

I first met Ann Whitman during the presidential election campaign of 1952 when she was personal secretary to General of the Army Eisenhower and I was a reporter covering his candidacy for the old *New York Herald Tribune*. For eight years after that, initially as White House correspondent and then as the Washington bureau chief of the *Herald Tribune*, I covered President Eisenhower and his administration and saw a good deal of Ann in Washington and on presidential trips. Later, when she worked for Rockefeller, she and I met off and on at governors' conferences and other events.

After enough time had elapsed so that one could appropriately discuss events and personalities of the 1950s, 1960s, and 1970s in a historical perspective, I asked her early in 1985 if she would talk to me for this book about her life, her work, her experiences in high places, and her countless private conversations with Eisenhower and Rockefeller. Now retired, she divides her time between New York and Clearwater, Florida. She gave me access to her personal letters and papers, which date to the Eisenhower period. I have also made copious use of her heretofore little-quoted diary of the White House years, which she kept at the request of Eisenhower to augment the historical record of his presidency.

Except as otherwise indicated, all quotations, direct and indirect, in this book that are attributed to Mrs. Whitman came from her interviews with the author.

CONFIDENTIAL
SECRETARY

1

A surprise awaited Ann Cook Whitman when she arrived for work one Thursday in June 1952 at General of the Army Dwight D. Eisenhower's presidential campaign headquarters in the Brown Palace Hotel in Denver. With the Republican National Convention in Chicago only three weeks away and a keen contest for the nomination looming between Eisenhower and Senator Robert A. Taft of Ohio, she had agreed to leave her job as a secretary at Citizens for Eisenhower in New York, where she lived, and devote two weeks to helping to organize the general's headquarters in Denver. But on her arrival at 8:15 A.M. on Thursday she found an unexpected message to report at once to the "Executive Office."

When she reached the small office outside Eisenhower's, it was obvious that matters were in an urgent state. Abbott Washburn, a public relations executive, informed Mrs. Whitman that the general's secretary was ill and could not come to work. And this was at a time when the headquarters was still struggling with a shortage of secretaries. Ann was asked to sit at the desk in the outer office for the day and answer the telephone.

At forty-four, Ann was a slender, attractive, smartly dressed, intelligent woman, the wife of Edmund S. Whitman, a United Fruit Company public relations executive and later vice-president. When Ann departed New York the previous Sunday, Ed—called Whit by Ann and their friends—saw her off from LaGuardia Airport. With him was a companion, Edward Bernays, the celebrated pioneer of the public relations business. A day or so later Bernays wrote to Ann, "You will bring such a gay and constructive spirit to it all." He added that "we are all sure that both Mamie and Ike will recognize all the values you have and are." The prophecy proved half correct—the half concerning General Eisenhower's reaction.

Ann had scarcely settled at her new desk by Eisenhower's door on Thursday morning when Washburn rushed back to say that the general wanted to dictate. Washburn astonished her by snatching her purse and thrusting a pencil and shorthand notebook into her hands, meanwhile half propelling her, over her objections, toward the candidate's door. She protested that she did not want to take dictation from Eisenhower.

"You have to," Washburn countered. "You are the senior person here."

As one of a group from Citizens for Eisenhower, she had shaken hands with him when he returned from his command of NATO forces in Europe early in June 1952 to enter politics, but she had not been introduced. In the summer of 1945 when New York staged a tremendous welcome for Eisenhower after the war in Europe, Ann went to the entrance of the Waldorf-Astoria Hotel to catch a glimpse of him. "When he passed he seemed to look right at me," she recalled. It was a familiar comment. Eisenhower had a knack of conveying to individuals in a crowd the illusion that he was looking directly at them. Ann had had no experience in political activity to speak of. A liberal Democrat, she had voted for Franklin D. Roosevelt at every opportunity. Of Republican politicians, she knew next to nothing. Like millions of other Americans during the Second World War, however, she had admired Eisenhower as supreme Allied commander in Europe and had taken the job at Citizens at the request of her friend, C. D. Jackson, publisher of *Fortune* and an Eisenhower supporter.

Ann's crisis outside Eisenhower's door was another matter. Because she didn't regard Gregg shorthand as her forte, she did not feel up to the task being forced upon her. Furthermore, as the two of them were strangers to each other, she was afraid to face Eisenhower under the circumstances. Nevertheless, as she later wrote to her friend and former employer, Mrs. Adele Rosenwald Levy, a daughter of the late Julius Rosenwald, philanthropist and chairman of the board of Sears, Roebuck & Company, Washburn practically "hurtled me" into the huge office. She suffered, she recalled on another occasion, "the worst case of jitters, almost I have ever had in my life." She was struck "with the dazzle of five stars." Eisenhower was, of course, in civilian clothes then, though his attire did nothing to alter the fact that, as the victor of Normandy and conqueror of Adolf Hitler's forces in the West who was now running for nomination as president of the United States, he was one of the most renowned men in the world. His office in the hotel was so long that he appeared to Ann as she entered to be sitting a mile away. Although, as she wrote to Adele Levy, Washburn "boomed an introduction," Eisenhower mistook her name to be Mrs. Whitney. Washburn left her on her own. As she approached the desk, the general rose and shook her hand. Without further ceremony he started to dictate.

"The first letter my hand shook so that I could barely write anything down," she later wrote. In fact, she virtually made the letter up. It was addressed to the widow of a general whom Eisenhower had known. "Then I realized," Ann recalled, "I could take his dictation and sobered up." Next came a letter to Eisenhower's close friend, General Alfred M. Gruenther, chief of staff at NATO headquarters. After that, Eisenhower dictated the latest draft of a political speech to be delivered in Texas, then a letter to John Foster Dulles, who was to be his secretary of state, about the foreign policy plank in the forthcoming Republican platform. "I also got the nasty job," Ann related to Adele Levy, "of writing the Texas speech on the big-type machine." The final drafts of speeches Eisenhower was to read were always typed in large letters to make them more legible. As the hours passed, she kept shuttling between her desk and his. "During the day," she wrote, "the general buzzed frequently, wanted clips (none on his desk); accepted the offer of a stapler; took a pair of scissors and cut up a stenographic edition of his speech himself; and redictated it to me later in the day."

"I came out some hours later in a daze," she wrote. But from that first day's work on through the next ten years, eight of them in the White House, she was Eisenhower's personal secretary. Yet if, before that first day in Denver, she had applied to be General Eisenhower's secretary, her résumé, satisfactory though it was, would not likely have landed her the job.

After public schools in her native Perry, Ohio, and a year at secretarial school, Ann attended Antioch College in Yellow Springs, Ohio, for three years, earning Bs and Cs. Then she moved to New York and worked initially in an obscure secretarial job. Following that, she was employed for sixteen years doing secretarial and accounting work for Mrs. Levy, a woman of outstanding achievement in philanthropy and community services. Though Ann's job was far removed from the limelight, it was exacting nevertheless and superb preparation for what lay in store for her. Later she worked for a time as a secretary for the Committee for a Free Europe, which operated Radio Free Europe. Last came her brief stint with Citizens for Eisenhower. Such a résumé, however, would have told little about Ann Whitman.

By the time she entered Antioch College in the fall of 1926, she was an inveterate, serious, and fast reader. Her association with Adele Levy gave her special entré to music, art, and the theater in New York. She had been introduced to Eleanor Roosevelt and was acquainted with Nelson A. Rockefeller. Among her friends she counted Ralph Bellamy, the actor, and she was a favorite of Edward and Doris Fleischman Bernays, Frank Altschul, senior partner of Lazard Frères & Company, and C. D. Jackson. She was a capable bridge player and occasionally rode horseback and played golf. In her mid-forties when she arrived in Denver, she was a stunning woman with brown hair bobbed around a face dominated by prominent cheekbones, brown eyes, and a wide forehead. Standing five feet seven inches tall, she had a gentle bearing and a graceful gait.

Her expression tended to be shy and quizzical. A colleague was to recall, "People didn't faze her," which drew from Ann the comment, "But they do—I just cover it up. I am shy." Nevertheless, she was comfortable and confident in the company of men. "I always got along better with men than with women," she once recalled, reflecting on her career. She regarded herself as a feminist, however. In the late 1940s she joined, but did not attend the meetings of, the Lucy Stone League, an organization that advocated women's rights. She considered herself a liberated woman two decades before the term became widely used. In many cases convention did not dictate her behavior. She was pleasure-loving, found excitement irresistible, and liked to drink and laugh. She had a wide range of feelings. While she had many friends, she cultivated only a few close ones and was generous and loyal to them. She was a proud woman, sensitive and dignified. Her style was formal. She had very definite likes and dislikes—of people and things. Racial prejudices offended her. In predicaments, as Abbott Washburn discovered, she could grow very tense, but without losing her balance. She had a temper—"quite a temperamental lady," Eisenhower once said of her. She was vulnerable to the pain of discouragement and disappointment. When she was tired or bored or was feeling the drag of an extra cocktail, she could lapse into a gloomy mood and become upset. Usually, however, she was resilient, quick, friendly, and smiling. When her work demanded confidentiality, her discretion was absolute under all circumstances.

On Friday in Denver, the day after her first ordeal, Ann returned to Eisenhower's outer office because she thought she was expected to do so. His regular secretary was still absent. Ann did not have long to wait for the buzzer. This time she was surprised to find that Eisenhower began his dictation while a barber trimmed his hair. As she noted afterward, "He remonstrated when the barber tried to cut one of the few remaining hairs on the top of his head by saying that Mrs. Eisenhower wanted them left that way." Ann was fully as surprised when the general spent a good hour dictating letters on Mamie's behalf, because—Denver being her home—Mrs. Eisenhower was busy with friends.

As one day led to another, Ann continued to work exclusively for Eisenhower without any instructions or intimations as to how long the assignment would last.

"This has been an amazing experience," she wrote.

In the circumstances, her ignorance of Republican politics was almost ludicrous. "I remember," she wrote later, "Senator Dirksen and other dignitaries coming into the office, being greeted enthusiastically by those more au courant than I. And I had not the glimmer of an idea as to their importance." The importance of Everett McKinley Dirksen of Illinois was that his support was a valuable prize being fought over by the Taft and Eisenhower forces. In the end, he supported Taft.

Certain things happened to her at the Brown Palace that Ann felt made a particularly good impression on Eisenhower. Once she awoke in the middle of the night, perhaps bothered by the rarefied atmosphere in Denver. Restless, she dressed and went to the office. While she was typing, catching up on dictated letters, Eisenhower padded into the office before dawn in his slippers and bathrobe, looking for something he had not intended to leave on his desk. He was astonished to see his new secretary already at work. Ann described a second similar situation in a letter to her husband. "He [Eisenhower] found me at work at 7:00 yesterday morning—which very much surprised him and he went around all day telling people. I *had* a lot of dictation left from the night before which I wanted to get done."

"Ann wanted to get to work before room service was in operation," recalled her former Denver roommate, Wanda Allender, later Mrs. Abbott Washburn. "She was irked that the

Brown Palace could not deliver *The New York Times* at dawn—*in Denver.*"

A third incident that, Ann later maintained, semiseriously, was responsible for changing her life, involved another letter to Gruenther. Eisenhower was considered a near-expert bridge player, probably the second best in the armed services in his time. Gruenther was an expert, conceded to be the best player in uniform. One night in a game with friends in Denver, Eisenhower was dealt an extraordinary hand and arrived in his office the next morning bursting to tell Gruenther about it. The technicalities might well have stumped a secretary who did not know the game. Because of her own experiences at the bridge table, Ann had no trouble handling the letter. She believed her new boss was much impressed with her knowledge of the game, which was to occupy no small part of his time as president.

Very soon an easy relationship began to develop between General Eisenhower and Ann Whitman. She wrote to her husband: "He's been darling to me—told me yesterday not to (when he buzzed) enter tentatively but to barge right in and sit down. I replied that I had hesitated because I was so frightened of him—he laughed and said—all·that bluster doesn't mean a thing."

To Adele Levy she wrote in June:

> He's really quite a guy, mostly serious, but with that flashing smile and ready wit, friendly, doesn't mind being asked questions . . . apparently completely sincere in his statement that he is not personally desirous of being President; somewhat surprisingly he stresses spiritual qualities throughout letters and speeches; somewhat scared and still bewildered by the change from military life.

As to the candidate's mood at that point, she wrote to Whit:

> The general is unhappy (off the record)—feels pushed around (and is) and put upon. Someone told him yesterday he should not play any more golf! He's more a slave, he says, than ever before.

Later she wrote to her husband that "again I am amazed at the stress he always puts on spiritual values. That is to me the most unexpected facet of his personality." To Eisenhower she never mentioned her reaction.

Her years of working in quiet offices had done nothing to prepare her for the turmoil of a presidential candidate's headquarters as the days wound down to the convention. In her earlier letter to Whit she said she had no social life "because all I do these days is collapse after dinner." The volume of dictation was so heavy that "I must be at my desk or have a substitute at *all* times (and this literally means going to the bathroom etc). My hair hasn't been washed—I need a manicure—and no relief in sight."

"But," she said, "it's still a wonderment that this happened to me. The hardest thing of all is what I *have* to do—that is, tell other people what *I* want—push them around etc. I still carry the feeling that *I* must be told what to do."

One of the leading figures at the Denver headquarters was Stanley High, who had taken leave as a senior editor of *Reader's Digest* to write speeches for Eisenhower, something he had done also for Roosevelt in the 1936 campaign. A short, wiry man, a former Protestant clergyman and editor of the *Christian Herald*, he had been brought into the New Deal to counter grumbling that Roosevelt was surrounded by Jews and Catholics. In another undated letter to Whit, Ann quoted High as having told her that "he has known Roosevelt, Willkie and Dewey intimately and worked on campaigns of all; that Eisenhower tops all those individuals by far. . . ." In one of the early days in Denver she typed a speech draft for High. After that on a number of evenings he waited until she had finished her regular work and took her to dinner, falling in love with her in the process. She thought of him as a "nice" beau but had other more pressing concerns.

Several days after Ann began working for Eisenhower word came that his ailing secretary had recovered and would return. When she did, she was quietly transferred to another office. Without any announcement, Ann continued in her new position, but she was uncertain whether she would accompany him to the convention, now only several days away. She wrote to Whit that "the tempo was building up (when we first came out I managed to get up to the room to change before dinner, etc; later we worked right through usually to eight o'clock, rushed down dirty and disheveled to dinner, back to work, usually out for a drink at about eleven, and to bed somewhat after twelve. And always up at four." On July 2, the day before Eisenhower's special train was due to depart Denver, Ann still did not know for sure what was in store for her until the general suddenly asked, "You are going to Chicago with us, aren't you?" She had to work until midnight that day, then rush up to her room and pack and get a few hours' sleep before taking dictation from the candidate early on the morning of the third. Meanwhile the hotel lobby had filled with Denver supporters waiting to cheer Eisenhower on to Chicago.

"At 9:45 . . . three of us in his office left for the station, he to leave 5 minutes later," she related to Whit."When we got out of the elevator at the Brown Palace I had my first taste of what it is like traveling with a celebrity. The lobby was jammed—with a lane left for us to walk through—a band played, we got to the station, got passed through a big crowd there, and onto the train."

Then her first impression of life on a campaign train: "You should see my compartment. I have two typewriters (one jumbo for [speech texts]); one whiskey carton full of stationery, your large suitcase, two smaller ones. . . . I marvel each morning that I manage to pull myself together."

Before each of the stops for crowds at stations along the way, High briefed Eisenhower, while Ann helped prepare cards with details for his talks. In Chicago she escaped the turmoil of work only once to have dinner at the Pump Room with High. Otherwise she was pinned down in Eisenhower headquarters in the Blackstone Hotel throughout the week, never even getting to the convention. She watched the climax on television, as Minnesota switched from Taft at the end of the first ballot, giving Eisenhower the nomination. She had never doubted what the outcome would be.

After the convention Eisenhower rested in the Rocky Mountains, and Ann and Ed Whitman went to Montauk Point, Long Island. When their vacation was over, Ann flew back to

Denver. There had still been no announcement of an appointment for her. Again it was a question of going where she thought she was expected to be.

"And the odd part of it is," she wrote to Adele Levy, "that now I am back everything is more or less routine—I've seen so much of Cabot Lodge, for instance, that it doesn't thrill me any more to be in the same room with him!"

Eisenhower, she said, "is beset by advisers and well-wishers. He shouldn't play golf, he shouldn't paint pictures, he dare not do this, he must go to church, he can't say that or this, or on the other hand, he must be his natural self. He is very irate about the no-golf regime that they would like to impose.

"Here," she continued, "you get caught up in such a maelstrom that to relax, even if given a couple of relaxing hours, is completely impossible. It's artificial and an electric atmosphere—but I love it."

In the remaining weeks at the Brown Palace after the convention she was intrigued with Eisenhower's comments during dictation. On August 6, for example, he was addressing a letter to Bernard M. Baruch, the financier and self-promoted adviser to presidents, in reply to a letter from Baruch regarding removal of Korean War economic controls. Suddenly Eisenhower hedged. "I better be careful," he told Ann, "this old Bernie Baruch is such a [Democratic] partisan."

Dictating a letter on August 12 to French Defense Minister René Pleven, a wartime friend, Eisenhower added a postscript: "I have not found anything enjoyable in the transfer from the military to the political world. Moreover, I have never worked harder than I am doing right now!"

As the lines were drawn between Eisenhower and Governor Adlai E. Stevenson of Illinois, the Democratic nominee, political tension grew. In both parties, as usual, early criticism arose about the way the respective candidates were proceeding. After the Republican convention, for example, the Scripps-Howard newspapers caused a rumble by carrying a front-page editorial saying that Eisenhower was "running like a dry creek." Frank Altschul wrote to Ann in Denver with a similar complaint. By this time her knowledge of politics and Republican politicians had expanded greatly. In the thick of the work on Eisenhower's speeches because of her typing, she understood his positions and knew everything there was to know about his campaign plans. She had become very much aware of what was going on around her, and her critical powers were in full play. On August 15 she wrote Altschul that a number of people in Denver shared his concern about the seeming drift of the Eisenhower campaign at that point.

"I am not denying," she wrote, "we have all had moments of discouragement."

While conceding that Eisenhower's positions were not altogether clear to the country, she noted that others around her discerned reasons for hope on two counts: "(1) because, seeing General Eisenhower every day, they are convinced, as I am convinced, that he is essentially, and in the best sense of the word, a liberal, and (2) because there are plans in the works by which he will make his position clear to the entire country."

In an undated letter to Whit she complained about the campaign organization. She said that "practically nobody outside the General has any idealism at all—no feel for the 'people.'"

After Labor Day Ann was so totally swept up in the whirl of the campaign that sometimes she did not know which state she was in. She was exposed to all the tortures of rushing to complete a speech typescript while jolting through turbulent air aboard a propeller-driven airplane (the presidential jet did not come into service until 1959), or dressing in a hurry with as many as three other women in the jammed stateroom of a train rattling along at sixty miles an hour.

In an undated letter to her husband from "Somewhere in Wisconsin," Ann said:

I have done nothing but work, and constantly—turning out great quantities of gush letters. . . . let no one tell you what an exciting life this is. It's hell. All the pushing, grabbing people in the world that want only to have their picture taken with the General—everybody out for publicity—and in my sourer moments, only three of us doing any work! The rest of the girls are young and pretty and out for the male element. I guess I am really getting old.

At Fargo, North Dakota, she got another letter off to Adele Levy, saying:

Really what an experience this is. . . . Discomfort, enormously difficult working conditions, being thrown together with a bunch of people—and thrown together on the most intimate basis possible— that you wouldn't ever meet in this world and probably won't again— long, sometimes impossibly long hours. And still I thrive under it.

The train is really awful and to my mind an outmoded method of campaigning. An ordinary day is 7 to 8 whistle stops—stops so frequent and so of a sameness that I frequently haven't the slightest idea in the world where we are, and a major or semimajor speech at night. A gala night is a major speech, which means part of a hotel bedroom and the luxury for a little while of a bath. Laundry is a problem that won't be solved until we get to San Francisco!—believe it or not.

When, on one of the trips, the train arrived in St. Louis, Ann announced that either she was assigned a stateroom of her own or else she would leave the campaign. She was assigned her own stateroom.

As to her approach to her work, she said to Adele Levy: "I'm staying strictly away from any partisan politics, don't you think? Only this—my personal devotion to the General hasn't wavered and my personal conviction that he is a wonderfully competent man hasn't changed."

"Whit says," she added, "I am so completely wrapped up in this that I could have no other life."

The train may have been miserable at times, but when the campaign was over, Ann admitted that the motley journey had been a great deal of fun, too.

At Denver, in the beginning, and then during the campaign, Ann became acquainted with another breed of men and women who were, inevitably, to remain on the fringes of her career for the next twenty-five years. These were the reporters and photographers who cover national and state politics. "Because," she wrote later, "Whit—and his brother—were writers, because I had always loved the written word better than the saying of it, because (and I must admit this) the press was brighter and lots more fun than some others in the entourage, I was drawn to their company." Over the years she made enduring friendships among them, notably with Merriman Smith, the famous White House correspondent for United Press International, whom Ann once described as one of her "special friends."

As the weather cooled ("today in parts of Minnesota, the trees had changed and the country was completely wild and beautiful," she reported to Adele Levy), Ann, who had neither the time nor the places to shop, became worried about her wardrobe. Through Whit, she sought the help of her friend, Mrs. Marie Clancy, a former colleague in Adele Levy's office who succeeded Ann as secretary. Writing to Whit from "Somewhere near Louisville," she said:

> Could you perhaps ask Marie Clancy to buy me
> 1 or 2 more suits—size 12—a dark gray flannel and maybe a small smooth tweed—
> also—a couple of nylon tricot blouses—size 34.
> also a black purse.
>
> Ann

One campaign trip thoroughly enjoyed was to Columbia, South Carolina, where the state's Democratic-turned-Republican governor, James F. Byrnes, entertained Eisenhower and his staff at the Governor's Mansion. In her letter from Fargo, Ann told Adele Levy that the mansion at Columbia "looked exactly like what it always did look like in every book I ever read. The mahogany did gleam, the flowers were almost too real, the staircase was a beautiful thing, and the trees were magnolias. What matter if there were two pieces of sheet music on the piano, one the Blue Danube?" But there was another and more exciting reason why she enjoyed the trip. In her letter from "Somewhere in Wisconsin," she related to Whit that the evening "was made for me when the General was being introduced to some Columbia people and they came to me and started to introduce me—and the General said, grabbing my arm, 'Of course I know Mrs. Whitman—she's my girl.' Gave me a terrific rating with the locals."

More people than the "locals" were intrigued. For weeks Ann's role had provoked curiosity throughout the campaign staff. Because nothing had been announced, no one knew for certain who would get the prestigious appointment as personal secretary to General Eisenhower. Still, it was increasingly obvious that no one else seemed even to be in the running. One witness to it all, of course, was Mrs. Eisenhower. At some stage impossible now to pinpoint, an incident occurred that has not been reported heretofore. And it still cannot be told in detail, because Ann herself knows only part of the story and those who knew more are dead. One of the principal officials of the campaign was the late former Senator Fred A. Seaton of Nebraska, who was to hold several important posts in the Eisenhower administration. Early in the campaign he confided to Ann that Mrs. Eisenhower told him she wanted Ann removed as her husband's secretary. Ann informed Whit in a long-distance telephone call.

Then in her undated letter to him, written in longhand on a couple of pages torn from a shorthand notebook and dated "Somewhere near Louisville," she said, "I don't know what will be the outcome of the problem I told you about—the Gen knows nothing of it—but knowing Mrs. E's power, I'm pretty sure I'm out."

An inevitable speculation about Mrs. Eisenhower's motives is that she feared the close working relationship developing between her husband and his bright secretary eighteen years his junior might get out of hand, or appear to. Appearances were very important to Mamie Eisenhower. To Ann, the thought was absurd. "Imagine!" she said to Whit. "At my age!"

The passions of the campaign had blown on the embers of old wartime rumors, reviving tales of a love affair between Eisenhower, the supreme Allied commander, and his secretary and driver, Lieutenant Kay Summersby. The full truth about that affair is unknowable, but in any case now the circumstances were utterly different than when Eisenhower was living in Europe while his wife necessarily stayed home. The revival of the rumors during the campaign surely awakened old embarrassments for Mrs. Eisenhower. Ann understood that and sympathized with her for it. Then Seaton again confided to Ann that he had turned down Mrs. Eisenhower's demand, if that is what it was, telling her that Ann was doing an excellent job and that her work was very valuable to the general. It is unimaginable, and Ann herself agrees, that Seaton would have taken it upon himself to rebuff Mrs. Eisenhower if he did not have the general's backing.

For all that anyone can tell, lifelong love, companionship, and ties of family pride prevailed between Dwight and Mamie Doud Eisenhower. Nevertheless, the great turn in Eisenhower's career in 1942, when he was sent to Europe and became supreme commander, inevitably caused their interests to run on different levels. While she was making the best she could of life at home, he was engaged at the heart of some of the greatest events in history, constantly dealing with the highest civilian and military leaders of the Allied nations. And now, in 1952, he was running for president. Mrs. Eisenhower did not share to any substantial degree in her husband's work, official interests, policies, reasoning about decisions, and methods of management. She was very good at the important social side of their lives in the campaign and later in the White House. On the whole, the American people regarded her affectionately. But she was not a participant in Eisenhower's professional life. By contrast, Ann Whitman moved so deeply into it that Eisenhower, on the testimony of nearly all his associates and indeed of his own, became very much dependent on her in a number of ways. It doubtless seemed to Mrs. Eisenhower that Ann stood between her and her husband where his professional life was concerned.

While Mrs. Eisenhower's apprehension was misplaced, her instincts were not irrational. If not by the fall of 1952, then with the passage of time, Ann Whitman's devotion, her affection, her loyalty, and her admiration for Eisenhower were so deep as to be

ALLEGHENY COLLEGE LIBRARY

all but indistinguishable from love. Yet she was never involved in scandal. This also applies to her long and close relationship with Nelson Rockefeller. She keenly resented what she felt to be Mrs. Eisenhower's unending animosity and suspiciousness. Even after eight years in the White House, when Ann was working for Eisenhower in his retirement, it was clear to her that Mrs. Eisenhower still did not want her around. This was one of the reasons why Ann changed jobs and soon found herself on Governor Rockefeller's staff.

Eisenhower easily defeated Stevenson in the election of 1952. During the night as the celebrating subsided at Eisenhower's election headquarters in the Commodore Hotel in New York, Thomas E. Stephens, one of Eisenhower's leading advisers in the campaign and his future appointments secretary, informed Ann that she was to be ready to leave with the general for the Augusta National Golf Club after lunch. Eisenhower had been a member of the exclusive men's club, scene of the annual Masters' Tournament, since shortly after his return from the Second World War. When the Eisenhower party arrived the day after the election, a small, temporary office was hastily set up for the president-elect and Ann at one end of the building that housed the locker room.

One day after she had settled down to work, she was notified she had a call in another office at the opposite end. Not realizing that it would have been better to go outside and walk around, she opened an inside door and found herself striding through the locker room just in time in encounter Gene Tunney, the former heavyweight boxing champion of the world, emerging from a shower with a towel around his waist. Recalling the incident years later, she said, "I think he ran." Sometime later Eisenhower, Ann, and Tom Stephens took a walk to look over some of the fairways, which had been designed by Bobby Jones, the greatest golfer of his time. After they had gone some distance Eisenhower decided to return to his office. An empty automobile assigned to the official party happened to be parked nearby. Ann piled the two men into the backseat and drove them to the club, an act that drew angry recriminations from the Secret Service. Now that Eisenhower was president-elect, she was informed, security procedures were strictly in effect, and henceforth no one but a Secret Service agent was to chauffeur him.

The president-elect and Ann were working in the temporary office six days after their arrival when he asked her rather casually if she would go to the White House with him as his personal secretary. She hesitated and requested a few days in which to think it over. The offer had not come as a surprise. Indeed Adele Levy had predicted it when they had talked before the election. At the same time Mrs. Levy had asked whether Ann could maintain her marriage if she moved to Washington while Whit stayed at his job in New York. From Augusta, Ann telegraphed her: YOU WERE SO RIGHT. THE QUESTION IS UP. NOW WHAT DO I DO? WHIT SAYS WE CAN WORK IT OUT. NEED YOUR BLESSING. Mrs. Levy wired back: YOU HAVE MY LOVE AND DEVOTION ALWAYS NO MATTER WHAT. She declined, however, to try to influence her friend's decision either way. Ann fended off the doubts Adele Levy had raised about the threat to her marriage. "As I rationalized then, and still now," she wrote thirty-three years later, "I could not have lived with myself if I had passed up the opportunity."

She accepted Eisenhower's offer. Was it because of ambition, a yearning for position and fame? "Ambition, never," she said. What then? "A passion for the excitement of life at the top," she explained.

2

In his authoritative volume on President Eisenhower, Stephen E. Ambrose said of Ann Whitman: "That Eisenhower could not have gotten through his task without her goes without saying. . . ." Of course, this is an exaggeration. No member of a White House staff ever is indispensable. Nevertheless, Professor Ambrose was right in calling attention to the ubiquitous role Ann played in the Eisenhower presidency. If any other female member of a White House staff has ever taken such a constant, voluminous, and vital part as she did in helping a president in the conduct of his office, history has been a long time catching up with her.

Bryce N. Harlow, counselor to senators, military leaders, and presidents, including Eisenhower, had his own characterization of Ann. She is, he said, a classic example of a strong, capable woman who works incessantly at the right hand of acclaimed great men and helps make them what they are without the public's awareness. The woman's own work is masked by the confidentiality her particular role imposes.

Ann Elizabeth Cook's origins offered scant portents of such distinction. She was born on June 11, 1908, on a farm on the main road between Ashtabula and Cleveland in the township of Perry and lost as little time as possible in growing into an intelligent, self-reliant, solitary child. Her parents were Willis Wood and Esther Few Cook. The Cook family had farmed in Ohio for as far back as Ann knew. The Few family had come from England. Ann's maternal grandparents, Albert and Hannah Few, had been married there on May 10, 1868, and almost immediately sailed to America. When the couple landed, they bought railroad tickets to the westernmost point their money would take them, and that was Madison, Ohio. Eventually they settled on a farm of their own a mile or so from the Cooks'. The 170-acre Cook farm had been left to Ann's father, whom she grew up to adore and who exerted the main influence in her childhood.

Owing to misfortunes, illness, and fears of illness, the household in which Ann was reared was not a cheerful one. Her father's widowed mother, into whose house Ann and her parents moved from a smaller one on the farm around 1916, went blind when Ann was a young child. Ann's own mother had been crippled by arthritis since Ann was about two years old, and her condition deteriorated. By the time Ann was twelve, she was able to carry her mother from the wheelchair, in which she passed her days, into the family's 1913 Model T Ford. Although Ann's father was to reach the age of seventy-nine, he was a hypochondriac. He was always trying special diets and some-times went to a sanitarium in Grand Rapids, Michigan. "If you were sick then," Ann recalled, "you went to a sanitarium." Her mother occasionally went to one in Oak Park, Illinois. When Ann was a young girl, she visited her there once for a couple of weeks. She returned on the train by herself with a note pinned to her clothing reading I AM ANN COOK AND I GET OFF AT THE STATION IN PAINESVILLE, OHIO. She knew nothing about things like birthday parties. "My father took me on little trips around," she said. "I enjoyed that more than anything." He had to do all the shopping for the family, including buying clothes for Ann. "He bought the most unsuitable dresses for a little girl," she recalled. "I remember one was yellow taffeta. I had no use for it."

Although other houses stood within a hundred yards of hers, Ann spent her childhood without any neighboring friends of her own age. From her middle-aged father's earlier marriage, which ended with the death of his first wife, Ann had a half-sister, Marion. But Marion was seven when Ann was born and thus too old to be a regular playmate for her.

The farm was run mainly by a farmhand while Willis Cook attended to other affairs. He was president of the local telephone company, a tiny one then. Though not a bookish man, he was also president of the local school board, which oversaw the education of children in a district with a total population of perhaps three thousand. He and—fairly surprisingly for her time, circa 1860—his mother had attended Hiram College in Hiram, Ohio. Cook was also president of a small school supply company in Painesville, several miles from Perry. Ann's judgment is that he was "one of perhaps five or so 'leading citizens'" of the township of Perry. One of his legacies to his daughter was an attitude of tolerance. "He was always ready to oppose anyone who tried to keep Jews or blacks from moving into our area," she recalled. After she had grown up and moved away, he ran for the Ohio legislature on the Democratic ticket but lost.

The Cook house resembled a comfortable middle-class house in an Ohio town more than it did a traditional American farmhouse. "There were no antimacassars," Ann said years later. The house was roomy and included an office for her father. The Cooks always had a housekeeper and sometimes a maid. With ample orchards and strawberry and raspberry patches, the farm mainly produced fruit; at times there were cows and horses. A sparkling creek flowed through a pasture, with a mint patch nearby. Ann had her own pony, Chief, an intractable animal. "He wouldn't do anything," she recalled. "If I would go out on a ride, he would decide to come home. And he did come home." While Ann was reared on a farm and acquired some knowledge of agriculture, her milieu as she progressed in school was more that of a small town in the Midwest. She did not, for example, belong to a 4-H Club, grow tomatoes, or enter prize farm animals in the county fair. She does not remember having spent much time in the barns or walking around the farm. Like all girls, she had dreams: one of hers was of dancing with the Prince of Wales.

Curiously, she did not go to school until she joined a third-grade class in the spring before the group was due to move on to fourth grade in September. "For a reason that I know not and always wondered about," she wrote, "my father did not send me to school until I must have been eight. . . . I do not remember his teaching me during that period, but I know I could read and write and do simple arithmetic by the time I joined the class. It was a one-room, three-grade school and I suspect my father felt I would do better at home." She has a recollection of riding to school at least once in a horse-drawn sleigh.

She also remembers reading an article later in an Ohio newspaper in which Marion was quoted as having described Ann as being a lonely child always lying on the floor reading a book. "Reading is a great defense against the world, you know that," she said many years later in retirement. "I think that is what I was doing. I still do it." Her youthful reading was undisciplined; she never immersed herself in the classics, for example. Yet she seems to have read everything she could get her hands on. Her father subscribed to farm journals, and she went through them. In his concern over his health, he also subscribed to Bernarr Macfadden's *Physical Culture*, a magazine Ann devoured every month.

Religion played a negligible part in her life. She was sent to Sunday school, largely, she supposes, because it was proper. Her father was not religious; to an extent, her mother was. There was a "great argument between my father and mother about 'joining' the church (a Church of Christ, I think). I think my mother won, but I was always an unbeliever."

In elementary school Ann excelled. "I soared through eighth grade, always ahead of everything," she said. "I got 100 on an eighth grade examination I took in seventh grade. The teacher did not know what to do with me." High school was different. "Until I discovered boys I was a good student," she recalled. The results then were Bs and Cs. "In high school I took a course and didn't open a book until the night before the examinations. I passed, but barely. I was arrogant. I thought I could do anything at that point."

The Cooks lived a mile and a half from Lake Erie. Ann did not enjoy water sports but used to go to picnics at Perry Park on the lake. Baseball became an enduring interest for her when her father began to take her occasionally to see the Cleveland Indians play. She watched such stars as Babe Ruth, Ty Cobb, and the Indians' center fielder, Tris Speaker, whose particular idiosyncrasy, she remembers, was to pluck grass and chew it throughout a game. "I knew everyone's batting average," she said. After moving to New York, she became a fan of the Brooklyn Dodgers and particularly of Jackie Robinson, the first black to play in the big leagues. Ann came to know and to admire him and his talented wife, Rachel, when she was working for Governor Rockefeller and Robinson campaigned for him among black voters. Ann still keeps up with current baseball statistics. In one way or another, sports have been part of her life. She was a member of the Perry High School girls' basketball team that won the Lake County championship in 1924.

Ann had wanted to go to a private high school and begged her father to send her to one, but he could not afford it. "I thought I would learn more at a private school," she recalled. "I knew nothing about nymphs and gods and goddesses. I never learned anything about mythology. When I married Whit, who had gone to private school, I resented that he knew so much more about that whole area than I did."

When she was a senior in high school, she could not decide which college she wanted to attend. "I don't remember that any of us had a goal," she said. "You just did what you had to do. If I had a goal, I wanted to get out of Perry, Ohio. If I had to live life over, I would like to be a lawyer. I never knew how to become a lawyer." Her father, like many other fathers in those days, thought it was wise for a young woman to learn typing and shorthand in case she had to support herself later in life. After graduation from Perry, therefore, Ann entered the Spencerian School in Cleveland for a year to study typing, stenography, and bookkeeping. She and a schoolmate from Perry used to take a bus to Cleveland on Monday mornings, board with an older couple during the week while attending classes, and return Fridays for weekends at home. Then in September 1926 she entered Antioch, with the understanding that her father would pay her expenses for the first year only. From that time on, she knew, "I was strictly on my own, financially and in all other ways."

At Antioch, students attended classes for six weeks, then worked at commercial jobs for six weeks, the alternating cycles continuing through the four years. The system provided them opportunities to prepare for a career and earn money to pay for their education. The first year Ann was employed during her work cycles in one of the college offices, so she spent all of her time in Yellow Springs, a town she found charming.

Soon after she arrived, she met a graduate student, an architect named Cliff Allen, who worked off campus, where he lived with two other men. "I spent most of my free time with all of them," she wrote. Although Allen was eleven years her senior, they became engaged. "It was serious," she said, "to the extent that I took him home with me one break." The engagement, however, did not survive moves in opposite directions of the country, necessitated by their respective careers.

Ann majored in accounting and literature and went on consuming books, helped perhaps by a speed-reading course she had taken in high school, one that stressed reading at a glance an entire line rather than concentrating on individual words. "The only literary taste that I developed [in college] and I don't know why," she wrote, "was my decision to start a library of books by black (then called Negro) authors. I remember Countee Cullen and Langston Hughes particularly. But that went by the board along the way."

Her sophomore year was a turning point in her life. Instead of being employed in a campus office, her work cycles took her to New York and a job as a typist with the New York Institute for

Child Guidance in the Hammacher Schlemmer Building on East Fifty-seventh Street.

She did a good deal of work for a man there who was also a professor at the New School for Social Research in New York. He drank heavily. One day a batch of examination papers arrived for him to grade. They had been done by students working for advanced degrees in psychiatric social work. Time passed, and the professor ignored them. Ann realized that the marks to be given would affect his students' progress. Finally she could stand his negligence no longer. Though barely halfway through college herself then, she took the papers, read them, graded them, and dispatched them to the New School in the professor's name. So far as she ever knew, the grades she gave were the ones that went into the students' records.

Two events, plus an infatuation with New York, diminished Ann's interest in finishing college. One was a decision by Cliff Allen to take a job in Chicago, causing him to break off their engagement. "I was devastated," Ann recalled. The other event was her promotion to secretary to the director of the institute, Dr. Lawson Lowry. It was an opportunity for Ann—more than she realized at the time because it also brought her into close contact with Dr. David M. Levy, a distinguished child psychiatrist who was chief of staff of the institute and husband of Adele Rosenwald Levy. Adele often visited his office and came to know the promising young woman from Ohio.

From her first six-week stay at the Institute for Child Guidance until the time when she made the supposedly brief trip to Denver to help organize the Eisenhower headquarters, Ann lived in or near Manhattan for some twenty-four years. Encompassing the close of the "Roaring Twenties," Prohibition, the Great Depression, the Second World War, the postwar epoch, and the coming of the United Nations, it was a time of tremendous activity in New York. Those were years of dynamic growth, artistic ferment, cultural change (for example, the end of the silent film era and the advent of television), and of an ever-faster pace in a city that was mistakenly thought to be going at nearly maximum speed in the 1920s. For a young, healthy, smart, alert, lively, well-informed, unencumbered, pleasure-seeking woman who yearned for life as it was not lived in Perry, Ohio, New York was a wonder world.

When she first came to the city as an Antioch sophomore, she had a room in the Italian section of Greenwich Village. At another time she lived briefly in the more fashionable Macdougal Alley, a mews a block above Washington Square North. She knew the small restaurants on West Eighth Street, along which in those days ran trolley cars, open-air ones in the summer. The "Els" were running then, too, and she sometimes rode one uptown. On occasions during her sojourn as an Antioch student she lived in small hotels or at a YWCA, in one case for $14 a week, including breakfast and dinner. After the stock market crash in the fall of 1929, Ann was reminded what was happening around the country by the appearance of men selling apples for five cents apiece on street corners. "The depression," she recalled, "hit all my friends, especially those graduating from Antioch. But I weathered it without a problem; I had a good (for that time) and secure job."

One of the first persons Ann met when she settled indefinitely in New York was Clarence Willard Moore, a businessman several years older than herself. Nicknamed Skinny, he had moved to New York from Omaha and worked for a subsidiary of the United Fruit Company. He and Ann fell in love, "and we did have a gay life around town," she wrote. Eventually they were married. Their marriage, although soon to be undermined, was to last for about seven years, but a good friendship between Ann and Skinny continued long afterward. Moore was dapper and a Dartmouth man to the core. He had graduated in 1921 from the Amos Tuck School of Business Administration at the college. At the time he and Ann met he lived at the Dartmouth Club on East Thirty-seventh Street, near Park Avenue. She refers to that era as "my Dartmouth-men period." "The Dartmouth-Princeton games were always musts," she said. She also recalled returning from a game in Hanover, New Hampshire, long before the existence of Interstate 91, when the narrow road on which they were driving was so smothered by fog that one alumnus had to sit on the right-hand fender and another on the left to guide the driver against going into a ditch.

The gay times during the years of their engagement and marriage were played out in settings very familiar to many New Yorkers of the 1930s and 1940s. On Sundays, Ann and Skinny often went to lunch at Charles, a popular French restaurant, near Tenth Street, on what was then called Sixth Avenue until Mayor Fiorello H. La Guardia had it changed to Avenue of the Americas in the 1940s. They explored the speakeasies. Ann's favorite one, equipped, of course, with a peephole, was on West Fifty-sixth Street near the Great Northern Hotel. "I loved speakeasies," she said. "They had an aura about them that bars do not have. They were a bit mysterious, and there was always the danger of a raid. We drank a lot—everybody drank a lot." After Prohibition ended in 1933, she and Skinny would some-times go to Lee Chumley's on Bedford Street in the Village, or to Billy's, a semifashionable saloon at First Avenue and Fifty-sixth Street, or to Zum Brauhaus on Fifty-fourth Street, near Second Avenue, one of the delightful old taverns in Manhattan, offering German songs and music from the operettas. Ann and Skinny danced to Guy Lombardo's band. Occasionally they went to the Glen Island Casino and to the summer concerts in Lewisohn Stadium on what was then the gravelly campus of the College of the City of New York on St. Nicholas Avenue. The first musical Ann saw was *Show Boat*, with a cast that included Paul Robeson and Helen Morgan. She went to the Ziegfeld Follies. Her most cherished moment in the theater, however, was Leslie Howard's performance in *The Petrified Forest*.

She and Skinny Moore were married by a justice of the peace in the Municipal Building in June 1933 and rented an apartment on East Twenty-first Street, near First Avenue. "Skinny's salary was, I think, $3,000 a year (he may have had some additional income) and we lived better in those few years than ever since," she wrote in 1985. "Flowers, a maid who cooked, a car. I simply cannot believe it now." Her car was "the love of my life." At about the time they were married the Commonwealth Fund, which supported the Institute for Child

Guidance as an experiment, decided to close it, and Ann was given a thousand dollars in severance pay. Realizing the dream of millions of young Americans who graduated from school in the 1920s and 1930s, she bought a black Ford roadster with a rumble seat and drove it with appropriate élan. Occasionally she would visit her father, covering the five hundred miles to Perry in a day, no easy feat before the building of the turnpikes. "I loved to get up in time to see the sun coming up over the towns in New Jersey and Pennsylvania," she remembered.

In the fall of 1933, after her June marriage, the basis of Ann's new life was shaken beyond repair. Her husband's best friend was Edmund Whitman, a colleague in the United Fruit empire, whom Ann had not met because he had been in Central America as the company's chief of public relations. On his return, Whitman invited the Moores to dinner at his and his then-wife's home in suburban New Rochelle. As Ann discovered, Whit was a man of dignity and substance, with a talent for writing. During his career with United Fruit, which had begun as a timekeeper on a banana plantation, he published four books of fiction and nonfiction, as well as a body of magazine fiction. His stories were set in Central America. Even his business letters showed a light touch. Writing to a friend about United Fruit's dividends and general financial strength, he concluded, "No bonds, no indebtedness, cash on the barrel-head, bananas for all." He was amiable and possessed the kind of quiet manner not always characteristic of public relations executives. Educated at Williams College and the Massachusetts Institute of Technology, he was the son of an army general and the grandson of one of the earliest governors of the Montana Territory. Whit was nearly eight years older than Ann, who seemed to have had a preference for men several years her senior. By the time the dinner party in New Rochelle ended, according to her, she and Whit were in love.

Ann and Skinny and Whit went on seeing a good deal of one another. Whit separated from his wife and moved into Manhattan and, in time, occupied an uptown apartment on the same floor as the Moores. On weekends they enjoyed golf and bridge games together. Ann and Whit's feelings for each other persisted. By 1938 or 1939 it was apparent to Ann that "my marriage to Skinny was over," that it was time for her to marry Whit. As he also was still married, two divorces were required at a time when divorce laws were very strict by today's standards. "At the time," Ann wrote later, "it was considered quite all right, indeed the thing to do, to get a New York divorce on completely trumped-up charges. None of us could afford to go to Reno, and that was the alternative—Reno or a crooked judge." Ann, Skinny, and Whit, therefore, descended on Yorktown, in Westchester County, New York (or somewhere in its vicinity), and told a judge a counterfeit tale of infidelity in a motel. "The judge," Ann wrote, "was about ninety (I remember wondering if he could be alive long enough to sign the papers). None of us had the slightest feeling of doing something wrong." Furthermore, "we all remained the closest of friends throughout."

Ann and Whit had to wait for something like nine months under the law ("Some law!" she observed later) before they could get married. He wanted the wedding to be held in an Episcopal Church; she did not. In the end no church would perform the service because of the divorces. But as Ann and Whit had reservations in Nassau, they "simply went there assuming we were married." After their return, they repaired to Greenwich, Connecticut, to try their luck with a justice of the peace. Unfortunately, Whit had already begun celebrating, and the justice would not marry them in Whit's rollicking condition. In the late fall of 1940, Whit suddenly decided to try again and called Ann at her office to ask her to meet him at Grand Central Station. "My greatest recollection," Ann said, "was what a pity— I had on the worst-looking dress I possessed, a sort of dull brown." But the wedding was performed in Greenwich, and they returned to New York and told Skinny. No one appears to have been unhappy. "We lived together, all three of us, for at least two summers," Ann said. Skinny married a woman named Ruth Berry, who survived him and for the rest of her life remained a friend of Ann's.

At first the Whitmans had an apartment on the East Side of Manhattan, then they moved for a time to Great Neck in suburban Long Island. In the war years they vacationed at Saratoga Springs, staying at the old Grand Union Hotel. They played golf and rode horseback. When shipping returned to normal after the war, to Ann's delight they took annual trips to Central America or Cuba on United Fruit ships, sometimes with the Bernays. On one cruise their ship left from Baltimore. When, on the eve of sailing, Edward and Doris Bernays and their eighteen-year-old daughter, Doris, arrived to check into the hotel, Mrs. Bernays, a staunch feminist, insisted on registering in her own name. The incredulous room clerk would not hear of it. For something like half an hour an argument raged at the registration desk, as Edward Bernays, their daughter, and the Whitmans looked on. In the end Mrs. Bernays had her way.

Already well along in her own disposition toward feminism, Ann's attitude was strengthened by Mrs. Bernays, who had edited a book of essays on women's careers, published in 1928. It was she who got Ann to join the Lucy Stone League and kept her in touch with women like Marguerite Clark, then medical editor of *Newsweek,* who were of like mind.

"In New York over a number of years," Ann wrote, "Whit and I were invited frequently to dinner at their [the Bernays'] home on East 63rd Street. Doris and Eddie rarely had just a purely social dinner. Usually there was a semi-prominent individual as the guest of honor (such as Howard Rusk), a sprinkling of their friends, newspaper and magazine people. . . . after dinner the guest of honor held the floor and talked informally, later asking [answering?] questions."*

Doris Bernays made sure that the feminist viewpoint was represented at the dinners, and Ann was attentive to it. "I had stood up for my own rights for a long time," she recalled. "I didn't rely on any husband or anybody else. I made my own decisions. I was never a clinging vine. Certainly, I was anything but conventional in my behavior."

* Howard A. Rusk was a distinguished physician, specialist in services for the physically handicapped, and writer for *The New York Times* and other publications.

On May 12, 1854, Samuel Rosenwald landed in Baltimore after a crossing from Germany. With a capital of twenty dollars he became a peddler on the old Winchester trail in Virginia. He was able to take his first step up the ladder, or so the story goes, when he had accumulated enough cash to buy a horse and wagon. In time, he entered the clothing business. His son, Julius, born on August 12, 1862, followed his father in that business and was prospering in Chicago when, in 1895, a brother-in-law persuaded him to buy with a borrowed $37,500 a quarter interest in Sears, Roebuck, then a company of moderate size. The mail-order business in the United States skyrocketed and so, of course, did Sears. "I had no idea Sears would develop into five percent of its present size," Julius Rosenwald said sometime after he had become a chairman of the board of the company. "It was simply a lucky chance that the business developed along such a scale." He knew what he wanted to do with his money. He became one of America's leading philanthropists and reared his five children in that tradition.

The second was Adele, who, in 1927, married Dr. Levy, the child psychiatrist. Although the New York Institute for Child Guidance was closed, Dr. and Mrs. Levy remembered Ann and her work as his former secretary. In the summer of 1933 Mrs. Levy called Ann, who had recently married Clarence Moore, and offered her a part-time job as her secretary. Then twenty-five and unemployed, Ann eagerly accepted. The job, soon to become a full-time one, proved a valuable apprenticeship for the White House. Years later in a letter to Adele Levy from Washington, explaining why she could not make a trip to New York, Ann said that at the last minute the president "threw a party of 150 people at me. The good training you gave me has pulled me through, or is working in that direction, I guess," she added. Moreover, by the time she entered the White House with Eisenhower in 1953, she had already spent sixteen years among the rich, the famous, the tycoons, the museum directors, the Jewish philanthropists, and the celebrities of one kind and another who flowed through Adele Levy's world. Ann was able to bring to her work for the president a familiarity with the manners, the attitudes, the expectations, the *ways* of many of the kinds of persons with whom he would often be involved by necessity or choice.

The setting in which Ann was to work from 1933 until 1949 was one of brilliance and luxury and of deep social, cultural, and civic concerns. A visitor to the Levy's Park Avenue apartment might by chance encounter Eleanor Roosevelt or Edward Warburg, both of whom shared in Adele Levy's activities on behalf of the United Jewish Appeal. She was the first chairman of the Women's Division of the UJA, organized in 1946. Her work for the care of children attracted to her home city health officials and settlement house managers. An occasional guest was Herbert H. Lehman, governor of New York and later a United States senator. From the theater came friends like Richard Rodgers, the composer, and the actresses Ethel Barrymore and Katharine Cornell, who was sometimes accompanied by Helen Keller, the renowned blind-and-deaf lecturer. Cited by the National Council of Jewish Women as the "Outstanding Jewish Woman of 1946," Adele Levy, described by Ann as petite and dynamic, was active in at least thirty-five charitable, artistic, and community organizations.

She was the principal organizer and main financial contributor to the Citizens Committee for Children, to which Mrs. Roosevelt also lent support. Being introduced to Eleanor Roosevelt by Mrs. Levy at a luncheon at the Gramercy Park Hotel was a shining moment in Ann's life at that time. Julius Rosenwald's daughter also established her own philanthropy, the Adele R. Levy Fund. She also invested in Broadway plays and musicals, including *South Pacific*. Her role as an "angel" yielded some delightful dividends for Ann. "Scripts came her way, which I devoured," she wrote. "Once in a while I either went with her, or on her behalf, to a 'run-through' of a play usually held in a producer's apartment or office."

"The finest of everything" was how Ann characterized the way the Levys and their close friends lived. "The finest furniture, the finest silver, the finest books, the money to buy all this, and the education to appreciate it," she said. Adele Levy's clothes came from Bergdorf Goodman, her jewelry from Van Cleef & Arpels. Servants were employed for every need. On the walls hung paintings by Picasso, van Gogh, Renoir, Cézanne, Degas, Toulouse-Lautrec, Seurat, and Corot. More than sumptuousness impressed Ann, however. "It was the *graciousness* of their lives and manner," she said. "I had never seen anything like it. It was a lesson I absorbed."

Trude Lash, wife of Joseph P. Lash, Eleanor Roosevelt's biographer, was a friend of Adele's and executive director of the Citizens Committee for Children. She recalled afterward that Mrs. Levy "loved celebrities, loved elegant people. She had savoir faire, impeccable taste."

"Mrs. Levy was an indefatigable worker," Mrs. Lash said. "She didn't just give money, she gave of herself. She knew she had political and social power and was quite willing to use it. She knew FDR and had stayed at the White House as a guest. When Robert Wagner became mayor of New York, she was often his guest. She was an extraordinary person, all generosity—a warm woman. Her sympathies could be aroused easily. She was forever giving presents to people. She would hear someone was in trouble. She would write a check for twenty-five hundred dollars—the person may never have seen so much money before.

"But if someone stepped on her dignity she was outraged. She was stern about being given her due. Her feelings were very vulnerable. Nelson Rockefeller hurt her when he didn't invite her to dinners for his WASP friends. A little foible, a weakness. She wanted to be tops in society. She was generous to Rockefeller in every way."

By this Lash meant that Adele Levy contributed to institutions and philanthropies in which Rockefeller was interested, especially the Museum of Modern Art.

Her personal affairs and correspondence were attended to by Ann at the apartment. Her various financial interests and those of her brothers and sisters were managed from a couple of floors of the General Electric Building at Lexington Avenue and Fifty-first Street. After Adele Levy made Ann a full-time employee, Ann worked mornings at the apartment and afternoons on largely bookkeeping matters in an office of her own in the complex in the General Electric Building. Mrs. Levy also appointed her secretary of the Adele R. Levy Fund. Ann would review and report to her on applications for grants.

"Once in a while, too," Ann recalled, "I was sent to inspect a playschool or a neighborhood house." She was not involved with large contributions. "I do remember being aghast at the method Jewish organizations use to extract money from wealthy individuals—by demanding larger and larger contributions at some public dinner."

Trude Lash recalls seeing Ann quietly entering a room in the apartment to consult Adele Levy.

"Ann," she said, "was handsome, well groomed, graceful. Her characteristic was that one saw her, but one didn't know she was there—such gentleness, serenity. Her office was so orderly, tidy. Everything was immediate. If one wanted something, there it was—no searching around."

Her future colleagues in the White House would have been incredulous. There her desk was in such a perpetual mess that not infrequently General Gruenther would take time out from his calls on the president to lecture her on the importance of a neat desk, all to no effect. Perhaps the difference was that her office at the Levys was just another one of the immaculate rooms in an elegant apartment, whereas her office in the White House was her own shop and the pressure was like none other.

But that was beside the point. A job, wherever it was, seemed to transform Ann. Once she took a job, the indifferent student from Perry High School and Antioch College, the laughing companion at Billy's or the Brauhaus, vanished. When she walked into the Levy house or the White House or the Governor's Mansion in Albany, all her talents focused on work for as many hours of the day or night as might be required. Precision took over. Error, sloppiness were intolerable. The wells of loyalty and devotion overflowed. Whether it was to Adele Levy or President Eisenhower or Vice-President Rockefeller, Ann's attachment became intense. Confidences were sacred. Her powers of imagination were harnessed to the next move. "She can keep one step ahead of you," Mrs. Levy said, "always anticipating what you'll be thinking next . . . what you'll be needing next."

Ann and Adele, who was forty-one—sixteen years Ann's senior—when Ann went to work for her, became so fond of each other and Ann absorbed so much of lasting value from Adele that it is a temptation to see a mother-daughter relationship. This is particularly true because Ann knew her own mother only as an invalid. Ann denies such a relationship. On the other hand, in one of her letters to Adele in 1952, Ann bespoke her love, as she often did, and mentioned "the need for your guardian's eye." The expression was in keeping with Ann's immediately telegraphing Adele about Eisenhower's offer of the secretary's job and soliciting her approval. In Ann's first Christmas season in the White House, in 1953, she was to write to her friend: "I do terribly miss the warmth and fun of Christmas at 300 Park . . . and most of all being with you and being sheltered and almost mothered for so many years."

"I am," wrote Ann, apparently in 1956, "totally devoted to you—and even after seven years and even at my age, I feel now and again like a motherless child."

By a previous marriage Adele had two sons, Richard and Armand Deutsch. Her sister, Marion Rosenwald Ascoli, the wife of Max Ascoli, a writer, scholar, and editor and publisher of the *Reporter*, a magazine now defunct, recalled that Adele always regretted not having a daughter. She adopted, as it were, "substitute daughters," Mrs. Ascoli said. One, she added, was the actress Benay Venuta, who was married at one time to Armand Deutsch. The other, according to Mrs. Ascoli, was Ann. What was there about Ann that Mrs. Levy particularly liked? "People don't seem to remember," Marion Ascoli replied, "that my sister was full of fun and merriment, and Ann had a very good sense of humor. That is one reason why she and Adele were such good friends." Mrs. Ascoli said that Adele had "real flair for finding the ridiculous in life and enjoying it." Most people who ever knew Ann Whitman would agree that that was precisely the right company for her.

One truth that struck Ann at the time was that members of a family may differ very intensely on a public issue without allowing the dispute to affect their love and closeness with one another. During the late 1940s she was exposed to a sharp conflict between Adele Levy and her brother, Lessing Julius Rosenwald, on the question of whether American Jews should support the establishment of a Jewish homeland in Palestine.

Adele, as a Red Cross worker, had inspected postwar refugee camps in Europe, and she contributed heavily to the transportation of Jews, especially Jewish children, from the diaspora to Palestine. She staunchly supported the main current of Jewish opinion in the United States in favor of a Jewish homeland, which, in 1948, was proclaimed as the State of Israel. She thought American Jews should assist Israel financially.

Lessing, who lived in Jenkintown, Pennsylvania, was completely opposed. He was philosophically anti-Zionist. In April 1943 he took the lead in organizing the American Council for Judaism and was elected its president. Its declaration of principles—principles that he enunciated in speeches, articles, paid advertisements, and testimony before official bodies—read in part:

> We oppose the effort to establish a national Jewish state in Palestine or anywhere else as a philosophy of defeatism and one which does not offer a practical solution of the Jewish problem. We dissent from all those related doctrines that stress the racialism, the nationalism, and the theoretical homelessness of the Jews. . . .We ask only this: equality of rights and obligations with their fellow-nationals.

The world over, in other words, Jews should be citizens of nations exactly as other citizens were, and, therefore, they had no need of a state of their own. The argument was rational, philosophical, and legitimate, although it was rejected by the overwhelming majority of Lessing Rosenwald's fellow American Jews, including his sister. Ann would hear Adele's side of the case stated emphatically during Mrs. Levy's telephone conversations with her brother. But it was the failure of the dispute to alter their affection and relationship with one another that Ann never forgot.

After sixteen years with Adele Levy, Ann wanted to do something different from straight secretarial work and bookkeeping. She and Whit were still living in Great Neck. Commuting seemed increasingly inconvenient. She decided not to work for a while, but her resignation was not the end of the friendship. Ann corresponded with her former employer for years. One of her many letters was written from Gettysburg after more than five years with the president and following a brief call on Mrs. Levy in New York.

May 24, 1958

> It was wonderful to see you. I think I have tried to say this before, never successfully and it won't be this time, but there is such an atmosphere of artificiality, of living strictly on the surface, of mistrust of motives of everyone (and I do NOT mean the President) that I

forget momentarily the depth and security and affection my former life contained. And then I see you and it all comes back in a wave of nostalgia that is almost too much to bear.

"Mrs. Levy was awfully good to me," Ann said in 1985, twenty-five years after her friend's death at the age of sixty-seven. "During the last few years I worked for her she gave me a Christmas bonus of Sears stock, most of which I still have. I loved her, admired her, learned from her, and was proud that she called me friend."

A few months of idleness sufficed for Ann, and in 1950 she was back at work, again as a secretary, this time, however, at the Committee for a Free Europe. The executives were volunteers who took time from other interests. At the helm was the highly charged C. D. Jackson, who was fascinated with psychological warfare and was to become President Eisenhower's assistant in that field for a couple of years. The executive Ann worked for was Frank Altschul, the investment banker and president of the Yale University Council, a consultative body.

Among others at the committee were Abbott Washburn and Wanda Allender, his secretary and future wife. They became friends of the Whitmans. When the 1952 campaign approached, C. D. Jackson urged Ann to go to work for Citizens for Eisenhower in the old Marguery Hotel on Park Avenue. Washburn already had agreed to do so and added to the pressure on Ann. One evening when the Whitmans and Washburn and Allender were going out to dinner together, the latter first dropped by the Whitmans' apartment for a drink, now that Ann and Whit had moved back to Manhattan. As Washburn entered, he called to Ann, "The Ike man cometh." In the end, she agreed to go with Citizens. Then the call for help came from Denver. She and Washburn flew out on the same plane. Jackson told William J. Miller, a colleague at Time/Life, that steering Ann to Citizens was the best contribution he could make to Eisenhower.

By Inauguration Day, January 20, 1952, Washburn had been appointed deputy director of the United States Information Agency. Ann entered the White House after the inaugural parade, made her way to the office of the president's personal secretary, which adjoined the Oval Office, and sat at the desk. When she stretched her legs under it, her foot hit a mousetrap. She had not heard that when the Trumans were moving into the White House in April 1945, they were forewarned of rats by Mrs. Roosevelt.

One of Ann's first letters from the White House was to Adele Levy.

From the mousetrap, which I discovered at approximately 6:00 P.M. on January 20 right down the line, this is a—well at least a— remarkable experience. When we came in that day, our office looked like a dirty apartment looks with a mass of furniture dumped in the middle of the room—and still pretty much looks that way. Great dirt marks on the walls, the furniture resembles something stored in the attic for many years, all pictures gone, etc. . . .

And the Cabinet Room, too, would shock your housekeeping heart to the very core. You think you should feel a tremendous something or other, but you don't and you worry about the callousness of your soul. The President's office, too, is pretty barren and depressing. . . .

I spent the whole day with Bill Simmons [the receptionist] moving the chair from the side to the back of the desk, the schedule from the right to the left, trying to get rid of the second blotter on the President's desk (Mr. Truman always had a second blotter to keep visitors from tapping their fingers!!!). Much of the time (like when we asked to have a closet cleaned out) we are told that it isn't necessary, the boy can find anything and what matter if there are five dried up old ink bottles and a candy cane there.

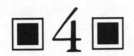

Ann's official title was personal secretary to the president, but Eisenhower more accurately referred to her not only as his confidential secretary but also as his assistant. For the mountain of work that this position was to involve, her starting salary— typical of the time but, by comparison, pin money in the federal government nowadays—was $7,000 a year, or slightly less than $135 a week. It did not change greatly any time soon. But Ann was excited to be where she was and did not complain about money.

Although of small dimensions, her office was surely the one of her dreams, being situated at the very edge of the epicenter. She was wedged between the Oval Office and the Cabinet Room, the site as well of National Security Council meetings, speech-writing conferences, and the like. The president would go through her office on his way to and from the Cabinet Room, often tossing off reflections to her as he passed. From her quarters overlooking the Rose Garden a few strides took her to his desk. When one of his appointments was over, he was apt to comment about it to Ann. He might, for example, comment to her about his problems with Senator Joseph R. McCarthy, the pugnacious, red-baiting Republican from Wisconsin, or say what his friend John Hay (Jock) Whitney was going to do with the *New York Herald Tribune* when he acquired it, or mention how he suspected that some real estate operators were trying to bluff him into paying more for property in Gettysburg, or explain how he himself felt about proposals for building a nuclear-powered cruiser. It was not surprising that when the writer Joseph E. Persico met Ann some years later, he found her to be what he called "a repository of insider background."

As Ann looked from her corridor door, just beyond the Cabinet Room lay the offices of James C. Hagerty, the press secretary, who had willed himself into looking like a bulldog by incessant growling, glowering, and complaining. The miraculous cures for this condition were Toots Shor's, Montmartre, an election-night Republican landslide, and two birdies and a par. Still, Hagerty was arguably the best of his profession, particularly important as a pioneer in dealing with television news coverage of the White House.

At the extreme left, as Ann looked from her door, was the lair of former Governor Sherman Adams of New Hampshire, who worked himself gray as the assistant to the president. He had quickly earned himself a reputation for rudeness and ruthlessness, yet he was flintier on the outside than on the inside. To those who were not either too terrified of him or too angry at him to see it, he was a strong and decent man in a very tough job. He was nearly unshakable, but, of course, that was before someone dared propose the admission of women to Dartmouth College, his alma mater.

The office closest to Ann's beyond the Oval Office was that of the ineffable Tom Stephens, the president's appointments secretary. In summers he opened his windows, which descended to the floor, and planted tomatoes outside. At his apartment he grew mushrooms in a closet. Unable to find pieces of wood on which to place the trays holding the dirt, he set each tray on four cans of vichyssoise, one under each corner. He informed acquaintances that he was having success growing mushrooms on vichyssoise. It was through Stephens's office that the publicly scheduled visitors from all corners of the earth passed to call on the president.

Thus Ann worked in the vortex, a snow white realm, which, despite appearances of calm and pleasantness, was eternally permeated with problems, tensions, conflicts, and often outright crises. Crisis or passing squall, what always mattered most to Ann were the wants and needs of the president. The interaction between them had developed out of the spontaneity and assurance of her responses and the confidence he felt in having her ready at hand to remind him of things to be done, or to transmit on-the-spot directions to others, or immediately to draft precisely the kind of letter he wanted sent, or to hand him, without his ever asking for them, the very papers he wanted.

"I was not efficient," Ann said long afterward. "My desk at the White House was always a mess. I would go off and leave my safe unlocked, and the guards would scold me. Mine was not the sort of efficiency displayed by keeping pencils in a row and that sort of thing. I think my forte, if you want to call it that, was that I was always able to anticipate what the president would need or what Mrs. Levy would need. I always had the papers she wanted or the president wanted."

Eisenhower relied on Ann to keep the machinery of his office running. After years of watching her work, a former White House male colleague, not a particular admirer of hers, recalled, "She was always a step ahead of the president." Hagerty remarked to Charles Roberts of *Newsweek*: "The president is devoted to her and is in many ways dependent upon her being around."

Around referred to many places, not just the White House, or the president's farm in Gettysburg, or his retreat at Camp David in the Catoctin Mountains of Maryland, or often-visited Augusta. She was with Eisenhower at ten summit meetings of one kind or another. Four were in Paris, two in Bermuda, two at Camp David, and one each in London and Geneva. She accompanied him to talks with national leaders in Bonn, Rome, Ankara, Karachi, Kabul, New Delhi, Teheran, Athens, Madrid, Lisbon, Casablanca, Ottawa (twice), Acapulco, San Juan, Brasília, Rio de Janeiro, Buenos Aires, Manila, Seoul, Taipei, Santiago, and Montevideo.

To be sure, she was not a participant in international meetings and sometimes had little, if anything, to do in the president's office during them. After the so-called little summit meeting at Camp David between Eisenhower and British Prime Minister Harold Macmillan in 1959, for example, she wrote: "I don't know why I am here, except that the President I think—and I do not think I am being vain—just likes to have me around whether or not I ever see him."

"He knew I was his friend, that's all," she said years later. On the other hand, on a great many presidential trips Ann worked until she was frayed. It was illustrative of some of the ludicrous confusions that overtook her on these travels that, as will be seen, Pope John XXIII unwittingly blessed her pajamas in the Sistine Chapel in 1959.

During those eight years no one in the administration other than she spent so much time with Eisenhower and talked with him as often. "I should also think," Sherman Adams wrote later, "that during those years she probably knew more about the details of both his public and private life than any other one person." Adams thought Ann "a proud and sensitive person" and admired her implacable sense of confidentiality. "This is one of the principal reasons," he wrote, "why she has not endeared herself to the Eisenhower family since . . . she was completely absorbed with the business and activities of the President. Not only were some of the family uncomfortable and even upset with the relations which Ann enjoyed with the President. There were even occasions when she was subject to impromptu and uncalled for comments and treatment which were undeserved and inappropriate."

"To my knowledge," he said, "there was no criticism of Ann's work in the White House."

Occupying the place she did, Ann was able to observe the

president in many kinds of situations and to judge his various reactions. The subject on which her observations placed her in perhaps the sharpest disagreement with many who have written about Eisenhower was that of his temper. She knew, of course, that he could be thin-skinned. "Criticism does hurt him, makes him unhappy—" she noted in her diary. On another occasion she listed in it things he disliked. She wrote, "Columnists, almost without exception."

She was familiar with his fretting over physical confinement in the White House. On February 7, 1953, less than three weeks after he took office, she noted that he "wanted to play golf, very, very badly. He awoke to a cold and drizzly rain. He peered at the sky frequently during the morning, and finally, after another excursion out to the porch, announced, 'Sometimes I feel so sorry for myself I could cry.'"

She was well aware of his grumbling over inconveniences like falling behind in his schedule. Thus: "The President irascible in a.m. because appointments piled up. Dr. Allan Kline [president of the American Farm Bureau Federation] was given some fifteen minutes—President said it took him twenty minutes to express any thought. Wrote Dr. Kline, later in day, nice note of apology."

Ineffectual subordinates, such as Charles E. Wilson, secretary of defense and former president of the General Motors Corporation, riled Eisenhower. "Pres. was terribly cross this afternoon," Ann noted on March 16, 1954. "Said Charlie Wilson has one-track mind, comes to him with all his problems. Said if he'd let him (Pres) solve them, all would be well."

Ann understood Eisenhower's capacity for anger. "He did," she wrote, "occasionally flush in what I knew was anger and a vein in his forehead would throb violently." Others saw the sign in the jut of his jaw or the icy flash of his blue eyes.

The stories depicting him as a man of fierce temper, however, Ann rejects as exaggerations. She never heard him use harsher language than damn or God damn. Through the door between their offices she never heard him yell at anyone.

"His moods didn't affect me," she said. "He was pleasant,

cheerful, gentlemanly. He never raised his voice at me. It was as though we were friends. He had a courtliness about him. I was never in awe of him. If you are interested in what you are doing, as he was, you do your job and don't get carried away with moods. I would say he had a rather matter-of-fact disposition. I don't know where this myth grew up that he was a man who vented his temper on everything. He was not."

"The President," she once wrote to his friend and golfing companion, George E. Allen, "is a politician in at least one meaning of the word. He really *wants* to please everybody."

When Hawaii was admitted to the Union in 1959, Governor J. Millard Tawes of Maryland wanted the first flag with fifty stars flown over Fort McHenry, at Baltimore, scene of a battle in the War of 1812 that inspired Francis Scott Key to compose "The Star-Spangled Banner." Learning that the White House staff had prepared a letter to Tawes rejecting his suggestion, Eisenhower asked Gerald D. Morgan, his special counsel, to have Tawes's request reconsidered.

"Later he [Eisenhower] said," Ann noted, "that it was so easy to be nice—and didn't cost anything—and he knew that staffs got into a negative attitude—but he wished they would realize how much is to be gained just by being nice."

As befit a secretary, Ann was well rehearsed in her boss's likes and dislikes.

For instance, the president once told Tom Stephens that his favorite song was "Ragtime Cowboy Joe," but Ann was aware that he also enjoyed classical music—"but is deathly afraid of being considered highbrow." He made a point of cursing motorcades through crowds, but secretly he liked them. He liked any army officer—"try as he will to conceal it." He liked royalty, but kept that a secret, too. He enjoyed seeing old Abilene friends and classmates—"for ten minutes." He liked editing. "He has many times said," Ann wrote, "he really should have been an editor; he passionately edits his own dictation and when he has time, every draft submitted to him. He once said to me in great disgust that 'the mark of a good executive, he supposed, was to learn to sign bad letters.' "

Eisenhower also liked yellow flowers. Ann had a particular reason to know it. One morning when she took cut flowers into the Oval Office as she usually did, he looked at the daffodils and said that yellow had been young "Icky's" favorite color. She remembers that on a number of occasions during his years in office he talked to her about "Icky"—Doud Dwight Eisenhower, Dwight and Mamie Doud Eisenhower's firstborn son. By the 1950s, most people had forgotten that the couple had had any child other than their living son, John S. D. Eisenhower, a West Point graduate, a major in the 1950s and later a second General Eisenhower, and who became a member of the White House staff under his father. In 1920, at the age of three, "Icky" had died of scarlet fever at Fort Meade, Maryland, where his father was stationed. "This was," Dwight Eisenhower wrote many years later, "the greatest disappointment and disaster of my life, the one I have never been able to forget completely. . . . The keenness of our loss comes back to me as fresh and terrible. . . ."

His dislikes, as Ann catalogued them, were pronounced: being interrupted when reading or working on a speech; "hovering, pestering, nagging"; protocol, and "having others say he dislikes his job." He liked it, Ann said, "but it would take a bit of doing to get an admission from him." Eisenhower did not like "modern" or "abstract" paintings; "women who cry"; "people who are 'afraid' of him" or "people who gush." Asked once to identify these last, she replied, "Delegations of Republican ladies and other groups of ladies who came to call on him wearing large corsages." As part of his West Point legacy, no doubt, he distinctly disliked "people who are too familiar," "people—politicians—who get familiar in a bodily sort of way."

Only the most obtuse Republican did not quickly learn not to slap Eisenhower on the back. His aversion to having people, especially men, become overly familiar physically was well known to his staff. One morning the Greek Orthodox archbishop H. G. Athenagoras of the archdiocese of North and South America was waiting in Tom Stephens's office to see the president. The archbishop, who wore flowing black robes and a headdress, was a large man with a bushy black beard. Just as the moment for the appointment arrived, an apprehensive Murray Snyder, assistant White House press secretary, slipped in and whispered to Stephens, "The last time he was here he kissed Truman." Stephens glanced at the archbishop's beard and darted into the Oval Office. Eisenhower said he was ready to see the archbishop. "When he saw Truman, he kissed Truman," Stephens replied. As the latter recalled the scene, Eisenhower said, "For Christ sake, why do you make an appointment with a guy that's gonna kiss me?" When Stephens escorted him in, the archbishop received a friendly welcome from the president, who shook hands with his arm straight out from the shoulder and locked at the elbow so his visitor could not get near his face. Yet even as the two men posed together for photographs, Stephens observed the president glancing defensively at the archbishop out of the corners of his eyes.

Above almost everything else, according to Ann, Eisenhower disliked lying—indeed was intolerant of lies. "An error made and admitted is forgiven," she wrote. "An error covered up by a lie is never forgiven or forgotten." In her diary she cited an example.

On February 1, 1955, I. Jack Martin, an assistant to the president for congressional relations, "proudly" brought to the Oval Office a letter from Walter Trohan, chief of the Washington bureau of the *Chicago Tribune*. The letter apparently contained "some kind of an olive branch" from Colonel Robert R. McCormick, publisher of the *Tribune*, an isolationist and a staunch supporter of the Taft-oriented Old Guard of the Republican party. Ann noted:

> The President would have no part of it. He said there were some things a man, even a forgiving man such as he considers himself to be, and is, could not stand. He said that during the war the Tribune had, among other things, accused him of being "the man who sacrificed American lives in order to cement relations with the British." That is a downright lie, and the President cannot forgive a liar.
>
> He said (Jack kept hovering around . . .) that the staff and the Republican Party could cotton up to the Colonel as much as they wanted to, but that he would have no part of it. He said further that Jack could tell Walter Trohan the President's reaction if he wished to.

Ann liked Eisenhower's military bearing and his laughter. "President Eisenhower had a hearty sense of humor as against a subtle one," she said. "He loved to laugh, but didn't pay much attention to nuance." She was always discovering new things about him. His detestation of crows, for example. On the farm at Gettysburg one day she and Eisenhower were sitting on the porch with two officials who were showing him prospective designs for rearranging the stars in the American flag after the admission of Alaska and Hawaii. Suddenly, without warning, the president stunned the two men by leaping up, grabbing a shotgun from a corner, and blazing at two crows reconnoitering a garden.

Although he kept giving her staggering amounts of work, she found him in other respects a thoughtful and courteous man to work for. She was impressed that whenever she went to see him, he would rise and so, of course, would the other men in the room. Sometimes when she was particularly worried about a situation, he sought to put her mind at ease. He was vacationing in Augusta in the spring of 1954 when the French were facing a critical moment during the battle of Dien Bien Phu in Vietnam. Under Secretary of State Walter Bedell Smith telephoned from Washington with some urgent piece of news. Ann took the call in her office above the golf shop where she was working alone because Eisenhower was away on a one-day trip. Smith gave her a message and asked her to go to the airport and hand it to the president the moment he landed, which she did. "I thought," she wrote afterward, "the world was coming to an end. . . . Later that night, the President . . . having talked to Bedell, called me twice at the dear old Bon Air [the hotel in Augusta where the press and members of the White House staff stayed] to tell me things were not as bad as I believed them."

Often enough, she saw him perturbed but never, she said, flustered, whether over a large crisis like Indochina or a small one such as that on November 4, 1958, when the president of the Supreme Court of Peru called on him. As was customary, the judge was to be presented by John Simmons, the State Department protocol officer. When Simmons missed the appointment, the courtesy fell to Tom Stephens. The visitor was Dr. José Antonio Eguiguren. Stephens said to Eisenhower, "How can I present him to you when I can't pronounce his name?" "Just introduce him as 'His Excellency,' " Eisenhower said.

Ann's attitude toward Washington as a city in which to live was, at best, neutral. In fairness, she once said, her negative attitude may have been due to the fact that she never gave the city a chance because she spent so much of her time working. She had moved to the capital in the midst of the inaugural ceremonies in January 1953, and housing was scarce. Whit got her a room temporarily at the Jefferson Hotel on Sixteenth Street, within walking distance of the White House. In the ensuing years Ann would visit him in New York when she could get away from work, which was not often. From time to time Whit would come to Washington to see Ann or else join her during presidential vacations in Denver or Augusta. During many of such visits, however, she worked such long hours that Whit had to seek his own diversions. After a period at the Jefferson, Ann found an apartment on Massachusetts Avenue: "one of those hideous 'efficiency' apartments that Washington so thrives on," as she wrote to Adele Levy. Then in another letter to her friend in July 1953, Ann said: "Work goes on much the same and I like it, and the President as much as ever. The poor man isn't, and I doubt if he ever will be, reconciled to the idea of being a prisoner—which in effect he is."

Ann did not always agree with Eisenhower's policies, although it was not her role to debate them with him. Two of the steaming issues during his presidency were civil rights and Senator McCarthy's assaults on the executive branch of the government. To this day his handling of those two problems continues to fuel the debate as to his standing in history as president. Ann was much more liberal than he on civil rights, especially in regard to the Supreme Court decision in 1954 outlawing racial segregation in the public schools. And at that time her sentiments were also on the side of those who argued

that Eisenhower should stand up to McCarthy and fight Mc-
Carthyism rather than, as he did, turn the other cheek in public,
maneuver as best he could against the senator behind the scenes,
and allow him enough rope with which to hang himself. Eisenhower gave Ann his familiar explanation that he would not
engage in running battles with McCarthy because the publicity
would only enhance McCarthy's power to make trouble. In later
years Ann came to accept the controversial position that the
president's course was the wiser one and hastened McCarthy's
downfall. In 1954 the Senate voted to censure him for behavior
unbecoming to the Senate.

She was always very loyal. During her White House years,
no one could criticize Eisenhower in her presence and expect a
warm reception. And many of the things Eisenhower did
aroused great enthusiasm in her. One was his proposal after the
Korean armistice of 1953 to have the United States Eighth Army
help restore the devastation of South Korea. Ann shared his
opinion that such an undertaking would win great favor for the
United States in world opinion. She was perhaps angrier than he
was when the Department of Defense and the American command in Korea conveniently ignored the suggestion. "The lack of
response . . . astonished and infuriated me," she wrote long
afterward.

The spectrum of Ann's feelings, convictions, and labors as
confidential secretary to the president was a very wide one.

She attended her first formal White House dinner when, as
she noted, Mrs. Eisenhower "very kindly" invited her to the
president's annual dinner for the judiciary. Nothing escaped
Ann's attention, of course. As she wrote in her diary:

November 7–27, 1953

*From the far end of the table, great fun; the President had hours of
the benefits to be derived from a salt-free diet from Mrs. Reed [wife
of Associate Justice Stanley F. Reed of the Supreme Court].*

She went to the first of the summit meetings in early
December 1953 when British Prime Minister Winston S. Chur-

chill was host to Eisenhower and French Premier Joseph Laniel at the Midocean Club in Tucker's Town, Bermuda. She wrote to Adele Levy later:

> Bermuda was, of course, a fascinating adventure for me. The stories about the security measures were all absolutely true—at one point I was held up on the porch for some ten minutes because, while I had my pass, the list said, "Mr. Whitman." The Fusiliers refused to be convinced. . . .

Eisenhower arrived with the draft of what he hoped might be a major initiative in slowing the nuclear arms race. It became known as the atoms-for-peace program. His idea was that the United States and the Soviet Union—he later added Great Britain—should turn over to the United Nations for peaceful uses an unspecified amount of fissionable material. The objective would be to change the focus from the building of nuclear weapons to the creation of better living conditions in the world with the help of nuclear power. Eisenhower wanted to present the plan in a speech to the United Nations General Assembly in New York on December 8 after obtaining Churchill's and Laniel's support.

Meanwhile, as Ann told Adele:

> I rather felt put upon because everybody else went out for calypso parties, etc., but I was stuck until the end of each conference (evening conference, I mean). Incidentally, I am completely in love with Admiral [Lewis L.] Strauss [chairman of the United States Atomic Energy Commission], who is a sweet man if I ever saw one. But Bermuda was lovely, the view from the window was, at least.

On the final day, after nearly everything had been packed and sent to the plane, Churchill and his military adviser, Lord Ismay, came down the hall at 11 A.M. and asked Ann about having a drink. "Luckily," she said afterward, "I had the sixth sense that day to leave out a bottle of scotch." She, Churchill, and Ismay got together with Eisenhower, and an attendant brought a bucket of ice and a pair of tongs. In making the drinks,

Ann found the ice cubes so large that the tongs would not grip them securely. "I was in a state of utter and complete confusion," she related to Adele. As Churchill watched her ordeal and sensed the danger of a lap full of ice, he said to her, "Just use your hands, young lady."

From Bermuda, Eisenhower flew directly to New York to address the General Assembly. Because of changes made in the speech after the president's talks with Churchill and Laniel, Ann and her colleagues had to work furiously on the final text aboard the Lockheed Constellation named *Columbine II*, after the state flower of Colorado, Mamie's birthplace. As the speech text still had not been run off by the time the plane approached LaGuardia Airport, Eisenhower told his pilot, Lieutenant Colonel William G. Draper, to circle New York for thirty minutes. The president, Dulles, Strauss, C. D. Jackson, and Hagerty reviewed the final copy, page by page. As each page was cleared, Marie McCrum, Jackson's secretary, rushed it forward and read it aloud, crouched between Ann, who was typing the reading copy in jumbo type, and Hagerty's secretary, Mary Caffrey (later Mrs. Thomas E. Stephens), who was typing on stencils. Once when Dulles wandered into their compartment Ann banished him. "You can't sit here, Mr. Secretary. We're busy." "While the secretary of state didn't actually wield the stapler," she related in her account to Mrs. Levy, "we shoved him around to make room for the stacks of paper until finally he was forced to hover up with the flight engineer. But everybody worked—no food until sandwiches on the way back to Washington [after the General Assembly session]. . . ."

5

After Eisenhower's staff settled down in the White House, the closeness of Ann Whitman's professional relationship with the president was a matter of note, even of surprise, for some of her colleagues. "Ann worked with the president with great confidence," said Bryce Harlow, a speechwriter and assistant for congressional relations. "She went about as the big person on campus." William Hopkins, chief clerk of the White House, recalled: "Ann was powerful because a request from her was supposedly a request from the president. It may not have been but you didn't know—you assumed it was."

The president's distinguished staff secretary, Colonel (later General) Andrew J. Goodpaster, said: "President Eisenhower often talked about 'getting into the other fellow's mind' or understanding his 'personal equation.' That was a strong attribute of Ann's, as well. She could see and understand what made people run. She could apply that to President Eisenhower, and he knew it."

Hopkins observed that if the president arrived for work on a particular day "on his high horse, Ann would reflect his mood to the people down the line." Goodpaster stated it somewhat differently. "An important part of Ann's role," he said, "was that she would know that something is troubling the president. She knew about things that worried him. She would tell us, so we could have a chance to see if anything could be done about it."

Officially, Ann's was not a policy-making role. Sherman Adams said later, however, that it would be "somewhat of an oversimplification" to say that she had nothing to do with policy. In Hagerty's discussion with Charles Roberts, he said that Ann contributed "a lot of good ideas." Adams, in effect, amplified that, writing "One of the particularly benign influences which Ann had was to throw out little suggestions to the President, and less often to me, about what she thought Jim Hagerty and I might consider with reference to some issue that came to the forefront." The apparent meaning of this is that she suggested useful ideas, no small matter, necessarily, when the White House was preparing to make a statement on some development. In journalistic circles in Washington speculation could be heard that Ann exerted what the columnist Drew Pearson called in her case "a quiet influence" on Eisenhower. Ann is noncommittal.

"I may have influenced his thinking, I don't know," she said. "I talked to the president a lot. I was with him more than anyone else. We must have talked twenty times a day. If he absorbed anything from my thinking, then I had influence. I can't tell whether that was the case."

Ann's close working relationship with the president, of course, gave her high stature. One colleague, Roemer McPhee, who joined the staff later on and became associate special counsel to the president, touched a not-unfamiliar chord when he said, "I felt a natural desire to stay on the right side of her."

If Ann went about, to use Harlow's expression, as the big person on campus, it was sedately. Her style seldom varied. On the other hand, though tending to be shy, she was also very direct. Out of tact she might refrain from saying what she thought. But if she did decide to speak, her words could, if she chose, be uncomfortably clear. Although she later regretted it, because her words troubled him, once in the early months of the administration she told Eisenhower that Dulles was the subject of much current criticism. She said that "people were critical of the impression Foster Dulles was making with especial reference to damage of prestige abroad and to bad morale in the foreign service."

At that point—she noted the conversation in her diary of November 2, 1953—Dulles was under widespread criticism, particularly for yielding to McCarthy's onslaughts against alleged security risks in the State Department. Ann's words reveal the candor with which she spoke to Eisenhower. Ordinarily a personal secretary to a president would hesitate before bringing up criticism of his secretary of state. She was sorry afterward that she had done so because, she said, her comment added to the miseries of a cold from which Eisenhower was suffering. There is no evidence, however, that he resented her frankness.

Years later, speaking in the aftermath of Watergate, she recalled that she, as well as others on the staff, had been quick to make sure that the president was informed of anything unusual going on around him that might cause him future embarrassment. If Ann could have prevented it, she would have kept him from being taken by surprise, even by a divorce, she said, without mentioning a particular case.

When the Nixon administration came to power in 1969, H. R. Haldeman, who was President Richard M. Nixon's chief of staff, terminated what he and his colleagues called "the Ann Whitman end run." Seeking absolute control over access to the president, a recognized form of influence in government, Haldeman, according to William Safire, installed his own assistant in the office Ann had occupied. To her furious resentment, Nixon's personal secretary, Rose Mary Woods, was moved to another office down the hall from the president's. What Haldeman was out to squelch was Ann's occasional practice of allowing herself to be used as a conduit through whom certain officials got papers directly to the president, who might not have seen them if they had gone through the processes of the staff. One of the three interior doors to the Oval Office opened from her office. If she felt that the president would approve, she sometimes let people in to see him on short notice when no appointment had been scheduled.

Members of the staff, for instance, might have wished to get a report or a letter or a congressional request to the president for his consideration without the delay of routing it through channels. They would hand the material to Ann in hope that she would see fit to take it into the Oval Office. To accompany such a document on one occasion Harlow wrote:

Indefatigable Ann—

Use, please and of course, your superlative discretion as to whether or not to *bother* Him with the enclosed.

And to *you*—how can you do all these things thoughtful tho' they are, amidst your endless travail?

Admiringly
BH

Ann occasionally provided access for Henry Cabot Lodge, Jr., then an ambassador and permanent U.S. representative to the United Nations. He might turn up at any hour or on a weekend and might wish to see Eisenhower without an appointment. Ann would let him in to the Oval Office or arrange to have him meet the president in the mansion, if the latter had already left the West Wing. This sort of thing happened with some frequency. Lodge would sometimes telephone Ann from the United Nations when he felt he needed instructions from the president. One night she took his call in the kitchen of the Peking Restaurant on Connecticut Avenue. She would try to get the instructions from the president and pass them on to Lodge, or else arrange to get him through to Eisenhower by telephone.

If Nixon's chief of staff believed that such control of access to the president by an individual member of the staff was a menacing grant of power, then it had to be eliminated and apparently it was, as far as Haldeman succeeded in arranging matters. Adams, who was Eisenhower's chief of staff, made no issue of it in Ann's case. She was on cordial terms with him and Tom Stephens, who, as appointments secretary, was primarily in charge of the president's schedule but was not always on hand. Ann would not have done what she did if the president had not wanted her to. "I was no wheeler-dealer," she said.

On occasion Ann took it upon herself to propose appointments for the president if she thought he would enjoy meeting a certain person and listening to his opinions. As she noted in her diary in one instance:

> *About a week ago Keith Funston, President of the New York Stock Exchange, had written the President a letter commenting most enthusiastically on his press conference remarks. The letter was so unusual I mentioned it to Tom [Stephens], who said that Mr. Funston was an unusually attractive person. On that basis I wrote a letter for the President's signature, which he signed [asking] Mr. Funston to come down for breakfast some day. The appointment this morning resulted—since the President kept him an hour and a quarter—and because of my own impression that Mr. Funston is indeed extraordinarily attractive—I think it was a good move.*

Early in his first term Eisenhower asked Ann to keep the diary to augment the history of his presidency. After eight years it totaled between fifteen and twenty thousand pages. It is an extraordinary compilation of quotations, observations, insights, tidbits, and routine business. For Ann it was no small task, because she usually did each day's entry well into the evening after all other work was done. She was also scrupulously attentive to preserving presidential letters and papers that might otherwise have been lost. These, the diary, and other documents now make up the Ann Whitman file, one of the most valuable collections in the Eisenhower Library in Abilene. Hence, although she was not well known to the public then because of the confidential nature of her work, her name is now familiar to historians, political scientists, biographers, and other writers working on events in the 1950s, ranging from civil rights to military policy. Very few serious books are written on Eisenhower nowadays without mention of Ann Whitman and reference to her voluminous material, especially the diary. Her zest for discovering ironic situations, her amusement over trivialities in high places, and delight in unexpected remarks flourish in its pages.

If the president cooked soup for the singer Mary Martin, Ann recorded it. If he paid a bridge debt of fifty dollars to his son John, into the diary went a reference to the transaction. If he told Ann he liked Walter H. Annenberg, publisher of the *Philadelphia Inquirer,* that fact was preserved for history. When Howell G. Crim, chief usher of the White House, warned the president after nine months in office that he was spending too much money—"$10,116 for temporary help"—Eisenhower's plight became a matter of future record. And into the record, too, went his comment, as applicable now as then (if not more so) in a number of cases: "I want to give businessmen an honorable place but they make crooks out of themselves."

He often relied on Ann to relay directives and information about his views to appropriate members of the staff. The record is dotted with such examples of her memorandums as:

Governor Adams

. . . Reminders for you are:
1. You are to check with Charlie Wilson about appointment of David Sarnoff to take General Adler's place on National Security Training Commission. On balance, President would prefer him rather than other suggestion, John Cowles.
2. You are to call Secretary [of Commerce Sinclair] Weeks and say President specifically mentioned him; understands of course that he did not come out here [Denver] because nothing specifically to report—and tell him President looks forward to seeing him.
3. You are to call Pete Jones [W. Alton Jones, chairman of the board of the Cities Service Company] . . . to arrange to have Mr. Jones report to Mr. Hoover [Under Secretary of State Herbert Hoover, Jr.] what he thinks is a formula for getting Colonel Nasser on our side.

4. You will probably want to check with Jim [Hagerty] and others President's suggestion of having Cabinet in for coffee at 11 o'clock Saturday morning . . .

a.

And a memorandum to General Wilton B. Persons, the deputy assistant and later the assistant to the president:

> The President said he did not "heartily approve" of polls that Congressmen make of thinking in their districts. He said he thought a Congressman ought to make up his own mind on subjects as are usually polled—and he mentioned defense—and stand or fall on *his* decision. I thought for future letters you—and the legislative liaison people ought to know.
>
> Ann Whitman

On the other hand, if she ever thought Eisenhower might want to intervene in some action about to be taken elsewhere in the government, she would let him know about it as soon as she heard. Thus:

> The President:
>
> Fred Seaton [assistant secretary of defense] called.
> Secretary [of the Navy Charles S.] Thomas has talked to him. Thomas proposes to release a statement tonight or tomorrow to effect that Navy will take advantage of selective service for the first time since 1947. The Navy plans to take 10,000 men.
> Thomas has gone all over this with Secretary Wilson; Thomas offered to come . . . here but Wilson said not necessary (with which Fred agreed).
> I send you this note now because the release may be made at 5:00 today . . .
>
> a.

After first calling his new secretary Mrs. Whitney by mistake in 1952 and then Mrs. Whitman, by 1954 Eisenhower called her Ann, or sometimes Annie, which her husband often called her.

In countless ways she helped Eisenhower keep abreast of the avalanche of details that descend on a president.

7/30

Letter to Bulganin.

I assume it should go by pouch (and that cabled version should not be sent). It will not arrive in Moscow until Tuesday.

In reply Eisenhower indicated "no cable version."

Reminder: John has a birthday August 3rd!

7/30

Bad news. You can't fly, visibility not good enough. Secret service, Mrs. Eisenhower, Jim, everybody notified . . .
Before I wrote to Cliff Roberts, he called me. Wondered if you would have an hour—suggested Monday.
When I thought it over, I think Tuesday will be better. It is saved for golf, maybe you would want to play golf with him, have talk and maybe dinner?

Eisenhower checked "Okay to ask him to come down Tuesday" in response.

[3/10/55]

You told me to bring you this file today; I think you want to say "No" definitely to request that you speak at Gettysburg National Cemetery May 30th.
It wasn't Richard Brown's name for stag dinner that haunted you, was it?

"Put him on," Eisenhower jotted back.

7/30

Reminder:
That you wanted to call, or have me call, Max Elban about fitting David to some golf clubs.*

* David Eisenhower, the president's grandson.

Frequently, of course, Ann's work was shaped by the exigencies of the day. But apart from spontaneous chores, it essentially revolved around letters. Basically, she was responsible for the president's personal correspondence, a major function in any administration. She had brought to the White House the novel idea, fully shared by Eisenhower, that the style of all presidential letters should be greatly elevated, a goal in which she was constantly frustrated by ancient bureaucratic practices in the White House correspondence section and typing pool.

Presidential correspondence takes many forms. Letters for the president's signature requiring particular expertise were drafted by his science adviser, economics adviser, congressional relations adviser, or special counsel, depending on the case. Such letters went to the president through Ann but were not hers. The rest of the field, however, was large and amorphous, and involved her completely.

There were letters Eisenhower dictated to Ann—and he would dictate to practically no one else. There were letters she would regularly compose herself for him to sign. There were letters she wrote on behalf of the president to which she would sign her own name. There were certain special letters she wrote on her own initiative for the president, which, if he approved, he would edit and sign. Then there was a great miscellany of routine letters handled by the communications section, according to ancient formula, models of monotonous jargon, which Ann furiously rewrote for the president until the task proved so time-consuming she had to give it up.

In the army and later as president of Columbia University, Eisenhower evidently had been accustomed to dictating all his personal letters, as contrasted with routine official letters written by his staff for him to sign. In Denver in the summer of 1952, Ann noted his style. "Paces the floor as he dictates; dictates rapidly with comparatively few corrects; and with emphasis . . ." After he was nominated, the demands for personal replies to letters became staggering. One day during the campaign there arrived from the widow of a French general whom Eisenhower had known a copy of a new book about the man. Ann took it, familiarized herself with the jacket copy, and then wrote a warm letter as if it were the handiwork of Eisenhower himself. When she handed it to him to edit and sign, if he liked it, he did so with surprise and gratitude. Thus began the practice, which was to become a fixture in the White House, of Ann's writing perhaps hundreds or thousands of private letters for his editing and signature.

On occasion, she wrote timely, purposeful letters to propose to him without any advance knowledge on his part. One night after work, for example, she and Mary Caffrey went to dinner at Duke Zeibert's old restaurant on L Street. Then Ann returned to her apartment and went to sleep, only to awaken at 3 A.M. Unable to doze, she got to thinking about Eisenhower's dismay over congressional opposition to a defense reorganization bill he had submitted. She sat and drafted a letter she thought he ought to send to a group of prominent businessmen to whom he periodically wrote, soliciting their support for some program.

"Ann had a feeling for how the president wrote," William Hopkins once said. Her opening lines in the letter did nothing to refute the comment.

Dear Mr._____:

I am sure it is no news to you that I am engaged in an all-out effort to secure legislation under which the Defense Department may be organized to meet modern security requirements with maximum efficiency and minimum cost.

After an analysis of the problem in the Pentagon as Eisenhower saw it and a summary of the remedies proposed in the legislation, the letter concluded:

I hope that you, and others, will find it useful in awakening the public to the grave seriousness of this matter. I am sending this letter, or one nearly identical, to a number of my good friends in the business world.

By daylight the draft was finished. Later in the day Eisenhower did some minor editing and signed the letter, and copies, dated March 6, 1958, were put in the mail. To the disappointment of the president and Ann, Congress ultimately passed a compromise bill.

On a host of other less important letters Ann wrote she simply signed Eisenhower's name. If Ann had a genius, it was for reproducing his signature with an exactness a counterfeiter would have envied. "But," she said, "the president knew about it and preferred I sign his name (rather than use machine signature) for the rather callous reason that, if necessary, he could always legally prove a signature of mine was not authentic whereas the machine was." She never signed his name to major official documents.

Over her own signature she would answer many letters written to the president that required substantive answers—answers explaining his position or attitude on matters raised by the correspondent. A rather interesting example of such a letter was the one Ann wrote to Dr. Arthur E. Morgan, who was then president of Antioch College, as he had been when she was an undergraduate twenty-five years earlier. Morgan had written to Eisenhower about the possible drawbacks of appointing partisan applicants to jobs in operating agencies such as the Tennessee Valley Authority. Morgan's letter had cited, by contrast, the practices of the British civil service.

Ann replied:

> The President asked me to thank you for your letter of March first. I'm glad he gave me the opportunity to write to you—and thereby re-introduce myself to you as one of Antioch's more undistinguished students.

Eisenhower had no quarrel with any of Morgan's comments, she said. But she explained that he believed he should appoint persons whose attitude toward government policies conformed with the views of the majority of the people who elected him. She concluded:

Certainly he hopes that our own civil service should be as free as the British system from what you call "political patronage." I know his efforts are steadily in that direction.

My warm good wishes to you,
Sincerely,
Ann C. Whitman,
Personal Secretary to the President.

P.S. Is the red bud as beautiful as ever?

The routine letters that were prepared in the correspondence section for Eisenhower's signature and that caused Ann endless anger and distress were mostly replies to citizens who had written the president to express their goodwill, or compliment him on a speech, or invite him to join some small hometown organization. Old regulations specified the wording of such replies, according to the topics of the letters received. Each reply, therefore, had an impersonal, even disembodied nature, because it did not refer to any of the wording in the sender's letter. "If only those replies would pick up one little thing in an incoming letter and refer to it," Ann said afterward. "Just one little thing! But I couldn't get them to do it." If, for example, a citizen wrote the president to wish him well or compliment him on some action, the standard reply, which sent Ann into a rage, was that the president "thanks you for your prayerful good wishes."

"Ann would say, 'What in the hell are prayerful good wishes?' " Mary Caffrey recalled. "Another example of the thing that would drive Ann right up the wall was a stock answer to a letter the president received from a youth group inviting him to join their Crime Stoppers Club. The standard reply that came to Ann was 'Thank you for asking the president to join. The president cannot join any organization in which he cannot actively participate.' Such a letter would have been a laughing-stock, Ann thought. So she threw it away and wrote a pleasant note saying that the president was grateful and wanted the boys to keep up the good work."

Ann remembers that for at least a long time she rewrote

twenty or thirty of these letters a day, sometimes seven days a week. She felt that a great opportunity in public relations was lost in the disembodied replies. Under pressure of other work, however, she had to give up, finally. The search for originality became overwhelming. How, for example, could one be original in thanking all the hundreds, if not thousands, of Catholics who, over the years, sent Eisenhower mass cards? "Mass cards drove me wild," she said.

Letters thanking friends of the president and utter strangers for gifts of every description was practically an industry in itself in Ann's department. The volume of such gifts doubtless varies among administrations. In the 1950s thousands of people, rich and otherwise, fairly flooded the war hero in the White House with presents ranging from nuggets of gold to smoked fish. Eisenhower seems to have been quite open about receiving gifts, many of which, like food and flowers, found their way to hospitals and other institutions.

According to Ann's records, Barry T. Leithead, chief executive officer of Cluett, Peabody & Company, sent the president a pair of pajamas. Not surprisingly, J. Edgar Hoover, director of the Federal Bureau of Investigation, sent a thumbprint ashtray. Jock Whitney mailed a Paris golf hat. A chamois rug came from Robert Montgomery, Hollywood actor and Eisenhower's television coach. Christiana Tsai's gift was the story of her life. Steve Napoli was the donor of pizza; Hickley Waguespack, of strawberries; David Beml, of bath accessories, and Colonel Robert W. Kenworthy, of two baseball bats. More practically, Martin Agronsky donated a sun dial and porch lanterns for the Gettysburg farm.

Ann once noted: "The President . . . was confronted with the overwhelming Texas generosity of Mr. Frank Wood, who wanted to send 200 chukars, 200 pheasants, 12 turkeys, and later 200 frying chickens. After discussion with Col. Schulz President will accept current shipment, but will indicate termination of such gifts."*

---

* Colonel (later General) Robert L. Schulz was the president's military aide.

Ann's labors over gifts were partly seasonal (maple syrup from Vermont fairly flowed into the White House in April, for example) and developmental, so to speak, as when color television came on the market. In November 1954, for example, Ann sent the president a note:

> Ray Scherer [White House correspondent for NBC] is very much on the spot about this new 21-inch color television. The usher told him Mrs. Eisenhower said you didn't use the present set, and to delay installing new one until you could find a place for it.
> He says General Sarnoff would be very hurt.* Present set is larger than new 21-inch set. You can keep both present and new one, should you wish. Can it be accepted even if not installed?

Eisenhower jotted on her note: "Yes, of course. I'll take it in office—& glad to have it."

The cornucopia never ceased.

"Eric Johnston [former president of the United States Chamber of Commerce and of the Motion Picture Association of America] brought in a new transistor clock radio that is a dream," Ann noted. "And in one of those rare coincidences that seems so frequent about gifts, David Marx [a toy manufacturer] also sent the President the same clock, and it arrived within the same hour. The President took one over to Mrs. Eisenhower's room and one over for keeping in his bedroom."

Although Eisenhower laid down what he considered appropriate rules for the acceptance of gifts, a spate of public criticism was heard over donations by rich friends, especially for the beautification and stocking of the Gettysburg farm. Robert W. Woodruff, chairman of the board and pioneer of the Coca-Cola Company, and others donated English boxwood trees and shrubbery. A number of head of Black Angus cattle came as gifts from friends.

In any case, the farm is now the Eisenhower National Historic Site, a property of the National Park Service, open to the public. Ann was one of the few people who knew that when

---

* General David Sarnoff was chairman of the board of the Radio Corporation of America, which owned RCA.

Eisenhower restored the farm, he had a "time capsule" sealed within the bricks of a main chimney. If anything should ever happen to cause the copper box to be found and opened, it will reveal various mementos of the time in which Dwight David Eisenhower lived.* One of the contents is a memorandum he dictated to Ann on foreign policy. The box also is believed to contain a candid assessment, written by Eisenhower, of the high Allied officers who served under him in the Second World War.

The task of handling thousands upon thousands of pieces of presidential correspondence of various kinds over the years would be enough to fray anyone's nerves from time to time, and Ann was no exception. Even in the case of the many letters she composed, the formal typing was done by others. A great deal of supervision, therefore, fell to her. She was stern about the appearance, language, spelling, and promptness of any letter that went to Eisenhower for his signature. Often junior secretaries were intimidated by, even frightened of, her and at times thought her tense, unhappy, preoccupied. Occasionally, no doubt, some young women were reduced to tears over her demands and criticisms, not all of which were always justified. "Ann could have an acid tongue if someone was giving the president trouble or her trouble," Harlow once remarked. On the other hand, a secretary who was left weeping by Ann's criticism was apt to be invited by her to dinner in a restaurant a few days later.

Ann forbade erasure marks on any letters typed for the president. When he received gifts given to him while he was visiting out of town, he wanted them acknowledged before he departed. Given the commotion of presidential travel, this rule could produce frantic scenes. Once in Newport, Rhode Island, the departure time was suddenly moved forward. Hence, though Ann had acknowledgments in draft, she could not type six

* Copies of the documents are in the Dwight D. Eisenhower Library in Abilene, Kansas, but at the late president's direction, they are sealed for at least seventy-five years from the date he deposited them.

remaining letters in time to board the presidential plane. She took six sheets of Eisenhower's stationery, had him sign at points on the blank pages where she calculated the letters would end, and gave these and her six draft replies to a junior secretary, who had to depart herself on the press plane a couple of hours later. The secretary, Anne Austin (now Anne Plaster), recalled in an interview that she had graduated from the University of Maine only recently and could not type very well. "That day in Newport," she said, "I had to arrange the margins so the letters would not crowd out the signature. Ann Whitman permitted no corrections on letters carrying the president's signature. It was a terrifying experience."

Ann's own worst moments were not those when the president had settled down to dictate to her but rather when he unexpectedly confronted her with sudden bursts of dictation on matters of immediate and large importance. Once the telephone awoke her at midnight. Eisenhower was calling to dictate certain instructions for Secretary Dulles, who was attending a conference in London. The president wanted to make sure Dulles received his message before the meetings resumed in the morning. From her bed Ann reached for the piece of paper closest at hand, which happened to be a front page of *The New York Times*. She snatched it just in time because Eisenhower started dictating almost at once, and she wrote furiously in the space over the *Times*'s logo and up and down the margins of the page. When the president hung up she was appalled at the thicket of her notes. Furthermore, her typewriter was broken. After midnight, therefore, she went to the White House, made her way through the bramble of her shorthand, typed the instructions, and telephoned the State Department.

She had another very similar but almost worse experience. Eisenhower was due to leave town early one morning, the date now unremembered, so Ann arrived at her office at seven. She had scarcely reached her desk when the buzzer sounded. Not seeing a notebook, she grabbed a three-by-five index card and stepped into the Oval Office to find the president conferring with Admiral Arthur W. Radford, chairman of the Joint Chiefs of

Staff. Eisenhower bade Ann take a message for the United States Sixth Fleet in the Mediterranean Sea, which he dictated as he was leaving for a waiting helicopter on the South Lawn. The message, no longer recalled by Ann, evidently was not of critical import. Still, it is in the best interests of all that any messages from the president do not reach the Sixth Fleet garbled. Ann managed to wedge her notes on the small card, but she experienced a moment of panic, fearful that she would not be able to read them. "But I muddled through," she recalled, characteristically laconic.

A duty Eisenhower assigned to Ann was, when she was not too busy doing other things, to don headphones in her office and listen in on many of his telephone conversations and make notes for the record. This was, and is, a practice common among high government officials. Ann sometimes heard some curious lines. On the morning of October 27, 1956, after Eisenhower had given a stag dinner, for example, she listened as he chatted with one of the guests, General Walter Bedell Smith, his chief of staff during the war and currently under secretary of state.

"President asked if he was too garrulous," Ann noted in her diary. "General assured him no, that he was wonderful, and that it was the unanimous impression among the group. Bishop [Fulton J.] Sheen left early and was extravagant in his cordiality."

"The president does love to talk," she remarked in a letter to George Allen.

To these frequent black-tie affairs, or stag dinners, Eisenhower invited prominent men, perhaps two dozen at a time, from fields as varied as corporations and labor unions, universities and newspapers, diplomacy and the arts. He received his guests for cocktails at eight in the elegant Oval Room on the second floor where attention invariably turned to his permanent display of jewel-encrusted articles that had been presented to him as gifts by the different Allied countries after the victory over Hitler. Later he led his guests downstairs to the State Dining Room. Conversation at dinner turned to all manner of subjects. Eisenhower was often remarkably forthright and candid. One night a corporate executive denounced Franklin D. Roosevelt with a vigor that seemed almost as if the speaker were saying something he thought Eisenhower would relish hearing. But Eisenhower retorted sharply to the effect that Roosevelt's high standing in the world had been a great American asset. Another time he talked about China policy in terms that, if stated publicly, would have made banner headlines. He expounded the sound reasons why the United States should recognize Communist China—at the very time when his administration refused to do so, largely because of fierce opposition from Republican conservatives.

Ann generally made up a tentative list for each dinner, perhaps after receiving suggestions from Eisenhower, Adams, Hagerty, and others. For probably few social affairs throughout the 1950s were invitations more earnestly coveted than for Eisenhower's stag dinners. Ann went over the lists with the president, and he made the final selections. If she felt strongly about someone, however, that person was likely to be invited. For example, Robert Frost, whose poems she loved, was a guest at her suggestion.

After the Senate, acting on recommendations of its select committee, censured McCarthy in 1954, Eisenhower was so delighted with the committee's effective work that he wanted to commend the chairman, Senator Arthur V. Watkins, a Republican from Utah. In the still-delicate political situation, however, the president was uncertain as to the best way to proceed. Adams asked Ann for her advice. She suggested inviting Watkins to a stag dinner. Adams thought it a good suggestion. Then Ann noted, "I suggested the idea to the president, who liked it." Attorney General Herbert Brownell, Jr., however, objected that such an invitation would, in Ann's words, "spotlight the thing too much." Instead it was left to Press Secretary Hagerty to indicate to the press the president's satisfaction with Watkins's work. A confusion of signals between the president and the press secretary, however, caused Hagerty to create a wave of front-page news about Eisenhower's praise for Watkins. It dwarfed the publicity that an invitation to a stag dinner would have caused, if Ann's suggestion had been followed. Three days later McCarthy apologized to the American people for having asked them to vote for Eisenhower.

6

In a confidential letter to Dwight Eisenhower's brother, Dr. Milton S. Eisenhower, president of Johns Hopkins University, Ann reviewed, at his request, the strengths and weaknesses in the way her boss used his time at work. Parenthetically, she deplored the fact that mistakes in presidential speech texts sometimes slipped through all hands on the way to the Oval Office. Once, she said, the phrase "consumer demands have not changed in 2,000 years" got past everyone along the line until it reached the president. "But of course he caught it," Ann wrote.

The ceaseless flow of paper throughout the West Wing offered myriad occasions for mistakes. Even in Ann's case never to have erred would have been inhuman. At times, however, she was blamed when she was not guilty. "I was accused this afternoon by both the President and the Secretary of State," she once wrote, "of losing the Secretary's suggestions for [Eisenhower's] televised talk. Ten minutes later they were discovered in [Dulles's] office, never having reached the White House. I drew a sigh and went on to the next problem."

On some other occasions she did not fare as well.

When Eisenhower flew to Los Angeles once to make a speech, "I managed to lose page 19, to his disgust," she said. She was particularly embarrassed because the discovery was made in the presence of her friends, Charles S. Jones, president of the Richfield Oil Company, and Robert Cutler, special assistant to the president for national security affairs. But Eisenhower "was nice about it. Later he scolded that I had not gone to dinner, which I wanted to but didn't know quite how."

In mid-May 1953 Ann gave Eisenhower for his signature a note that she herself had not typed but that she had passed. He signed it, and it was mailed. The note was as follows:

> The White House
> Washington, D.C.
>
> Dear Admiral Joy:
>
> Mrs. Eisenhower and I had a delightful visit to the Naval Academy on Sunday. We send you and Mrs. McCormick our deepest thanks for your warm hospitality.
>
> With best wishes,
>
> Sincerely,
> Dwight D. Eisenhower
>
> Vice Admiral Turner Joy
> United States Naval Academy
> Annapolis, Maryland
>
> P.S. And apologies for my brand of golf.

Any number of statements by a president have the potential for creating an international outcry or arousing domestic strife. This letter might have riddled the navy with gossip. Mrs. McCormick was the wife of Admiral Lynde D. McCormick, supreme commander of NATO naval forces. The McCormicks had attended the affair at Annapolis. When the boner was discovered in the White House sometime later, Eisenhower wrote to Admiral Joy again, saying:

My secretaries are shattered and I am contrite. I do hope that both you and Mrs. Joy will find it possible to forgive the error in my letter to you of May 19th. That I should thus repay your delightful hospitality horrifies me.

In fact, Eisenhower was rather amused by the contretemps, Ann remembers. She was not. It became her practice on most Saturday afternoons and Sundays to work alone at her desk, checking and rewriting letters typed for her signature or his.

Another time she had worked hard on a letter for him to sign. He edited it and signed the formal copy. Bill Hopkins gave it priority in the communications room. When the letter came back to Ann for mailing, just as the president was departing on a trip, she discovered that she had written "principal" instead of "principle." "I said, 'The hell with it,' and mailed it," she recalled.

After Eisenhower had been dictating letters for Winston Churchill to her, off and on, for two years, she suddenly awoke to the woeful realization that she had been spelling Cyprus "Cypress," as in Cypress Point, California. And Churchill, she once said, "was my god!"

She had another encounter with her god on June 26, 1954, that brought her momentarily to the edge of panic. The prime minister, on a visit to Washington, had an appointment scheduled with the president for the White House that morning. Eisenhower was already at work and Ann was with him at his desk when a buzzer notified them that the visitor was on the way to the Oval Office. Eisenhower stood up and said he was going to the bathroom. Aghast, Ann said he could not leave the room then. ("Imagine my telling the president of the United States he couldn't go to the bathroom!" she mused when she thought about it thirty years later.) Nevertheless, Eisenhower disappeared, and Sir Winston entered, confronting the solitary secretary, who had had not the slightest chance to think how to welcome the prime minister to the White House. If she had spent a year in preparing at the State Department protocol office, she could not have done better, as it turned out, than uttering, to use her words, "the first thing that popped into my mind."

"Oh, what a *beautiful* suit!" she exclaimed, looking at his white linen double-breasted jacket. He melted.

"He beamed on me," she hastened to write to Adele Levy, "and said he had got it for Jamaica a couple of years ago, and we were off on the Washington weather in leaps and bounds.

"He really is an old duck," she went on, "and no matter how difficult it is to deal with him [officially], I hope he lives on forever as the Prime Minister of Great Britain."

Later she found herself alone with him again.

"He asked me," Ann related, "if I knew a Miss Portal, one of his secretaries. I said no, and he said he would send her over. 'She has quite a pedigree,' and he cited it, and then said, 'she's very well connected.' I was on the verge of saying I wasn't connected at all when the Boss came back in the office and I was pressed into the scotch and soda, very weak, routine. (Actually Churchill's a great bluffer, he orders, but doesn't drink the darn things, and his cigar smoking, too, is an act.) . . . I got a terrific thrill a couple of hours ago out of forging the Boss's initials to a note to him to go to the British Embassy just before he left.

"You try typing a dozen copies of something that the President and the Prime Minister are impatiently waiting for and you get the most awful butterflies."

At the end of the visit, during which Churchill and Sir Anthony Eden, the British foreign secretary, stayed overnight at the White House, Ann had occasion to leave on Eisenhower's desk one of the queries she frequently jotted to him to get a prompt answer without having to break into one of his appointments.

Problem
Mr. Colville asked me confidentially how much the Prime Minister and Mr. Eden should leave as tips.*
I asked Mr. Crim; he says [White House employees] are directed to say that nothing is expected, but he said the Emperor of Ethiopia left $400—some other recent visitors $100. He suggested $100 each from Prime Minister and Mr. Eden
Tom [Stephens] and Jim [Hagerty] suggest I better ask you—

* Sir John Colville was private secretary to Churchill.

Eisenhower returned the query with a notation:

Total of $200 for party would be *more than* ample.

D

By 1954 Ann had been getting some fairly large doses of Gettysburg and Augusta, and they were not her favorite medicines. Gettysburg—"Siberia," she once called it—was, she reported to Adele Levy, "grim and gray, and utterly unreachable from the outside world." Augusta, she added, as "a town about which I can find absolutely nothing favorable to say." (Nowadays, of course, a locomotive could not pull Ann away from her television set when a Masters' Tournament is on. She glories in the pine and dogwood and undulating fairways she could see from her office above the golf shop.) When President Eisenhower was in Augusta, members of the White House staff and the press stayed in the Bon Air Hotel several miles from the Augusta National Golf Club, where President and Mrs. Eisenhower had a "cottage" on the golf course. The worst misery any reporter or any secretary could have wished upon the president would have been to swap quarters. The management of the Bon Air boasted that it had been a center of social life in Augusta when President William Howard Taft used to visit the city. Between the Taft and the Eisenhower administrations, however, something went seriously wrong. On New Year's Day, 1954, Ann wrote to Adele:

> We have fought, for instance, a losing battle trying to turn the heat off in our rooms . . . one of the girls has a bathroom that gives only hot water (red hot water) from both spigots.* The food is completely vile. Room service is nonexistent. It seems that the smart people who want breakfast in their rooms stand in the corridor and if a waiter comes along with a tray, slip him a $5 bill and make off with the tray.

And work was no frolic.

* The water in Sherman Adams's toilet was scalding.

Days we spent out at the club, in a little, but nice, two-by-four office. The President comes in for one to four hours in the morning, and then disappears for the rest of the day, while I try to crawl out from under. For one thing he got the nice, but wearing (to me), idea of writing appreciation letters (two-page affairs) to all the leading governmental figures. That took time!

The strategies through which reporters, photographers, sound men, the Secret Service, and the White House staff tried to fight off boredom at night in the Bon Air were the subject of another letter to Mrs. Levy on June 17, 1954.

"You might be amused," Ann wrote, "by a report on our [recent] Augusta trip—and the fact that for the time being at least we have conquered that dreadful city and awful hotel. We organized a series of 'guest' cook nights (and we had a small stove and icebox in the suite that Tom Stephens and I adjoin [from opposite directions]). So almost every night we had newspaper men and *Columbine* crew and photographers and signal corps and secret service men in to dinner. (And we had a "guest bartender' arrangement, of course!) So—we had a Japanese night with costumes and sound effects—(George Herman—CBS); barbecue chicken night (Secret Service); spaghetti and meatballs (one of the *Columbine* crew who is an Italian)—and so on. With much fun and good friendship. And I might say no elegance and no, practically no, silver or dishes. But it did overcome that dreadful emptiness and horror that is Augusta."

Christmas in Augusta with the president! What a secretary might not do for the chance! Ann painted the picture in another letter to Adele on December 26, 1954.

"Christmas Eve we had a party—I venture some 75 to 100— and served steaks (only they were cut into finger-thin strips which you had to eat with your fingers, no napkins) and a wassail bowl which did in some of the most hardy members of the press corps. Yesterday—I tell you because it is really amusing— Christmas Day, I had meatballs in an Italian joint for lunch, and a few slices of turkey, and that is all, just before I went to bed. Ah, the spirit of the holiday season."

*　　*　　*

In the letter Ann had written to Adele six months after going to work in the White House, she commented on how much there was for her still to learn about politics, politicians, and legislative procedures. She became, at the same time, ever more caught up in the political passions of Washington. As a New Deal enthusiast in the Roosevelt era, she never had much use for Old Guard Republicans, naturally, and her distaste intensified in 1952 when they supported Taft and opposed Eisenhower. Eisenhower himself was shocked and angered as a large number of right-wing Republicans, notably McCarthy, of course, remained hostile to many of his administration's policies. Ann shared his feelings. In a letter to Adele on June 17, 1954, she said:

> Matters political have been exceedingly depressing. My loyalty and devotion to the Boss have increased, if that is possible for such a thing to happen; my allegiance, if any, to certain aspects of the Republican Party has deteriorated rapidly and steadily. It is a decidedly unhappy situation. I fight in my own small way—and that you may be sure of.

Ann's job was her school for politics. She learned rapidly. The lessons came up day by day, and her diary is sprinkled with accounts of them.

She was with Eisenhower one day when Gerald Morgan, his special counsel, came in and asked him to sign a local Texas district water bill of immediate interest to the district's Democratic representative in the House, Speaker Sam Rayburn. Eisenhower tartly asked why he should sign the measure when the administration's Fryingpan-Arkansas water project, approved by the Senate, had been defeated in the Democratic-controlled House.

"Jerry pointed out instead," Ann noted, "that Mr. Rayburn had helped with foreign aid, etc.

"President very reluctantly signed."

Another time Eisenhower brought up with Ann the subject of an appropriations bill for the Department of Health, Education, and Welfare (now the Department of Health and Human

Services). He explained to her that the bill provided for more research funds than could be spent in view of the department's existing facilities and personnel. Ann supposed, therefore, that he was going to veto it.

"But," her note continued, "the President felt that the country would not understand—that the people were so aroused about cancer and heart disease and other things, that it would be felt he was heartless (that is not the word he used) and unaware or not concerned about the welfare of the citizens if he did in fact veto the bill. So another substitute message was prepared—he signed the bill but pointed out its faults."

Another lesson noted in her diary:

The President distressed at the Republican members of Congress who vote against him; asked me to be sure that anyone that asks a favor for a constituent or himself—that his voting record is attached to the request as it comes to him for decision.

Now and then, Ann's grasp of congressional humors slipped, as in the case of Representative Charles A. Halleck, a Republican from Indiana. He was, Ann noted, the most effective Republican worker in the House on behalf of Eisenhower's programs. Yet he was very gloomy because it was not he but Representative Joseph W. Martin, Jr., of Massachusetts, formerly Speaker of the House, who was the Republican leader. Halleck, therefore, was given appointments with the president just to lift his morale.

"Every so often," Ann wrote in her diary, "the President is called upon to pat him on the back. What I don't understand is that he is the only Congressman who plays golf regularly with the President and what better morale booster would there be than that?"

A fair question. The answer is a coup that would overturn Joe Martin and put Charlie Halleck in the official role of Republican leader of the House of Representatives. That is precisely what Halleck sprang on January 6, 1959.

One day Ann's political lesson was hand-delivered to her at the White House from none other than Leonard W. Hall, the Republican national chairman.

REPUBLICAN NATIONAL COMMITTEE
March 1, 1955

Memorandum

To: Mrs. Ann Whitman
From: Leonard Hall
Re: Robert Rex and Edward Durell

At the stag dinner the other night I sat between Mr. Rex and Mr. Durell and discussed with them the Ohio plan, and what, with some revisions, has been named the Los Angeles plan (under Mr. Charles S. Jones of Richfield Oil).

In a few words, the Ohio plan is simply this: The executives of plants and industries are organized on a non-partisan effort to get out the vote, the gimmick in our favor being that such organization plans take place only in those areas where the Republican vote is preponderant.

The plan has worked splendidly in Ohio and also in Los Angeles. . . .

It was not Hall, however, who was Ann's political tutor, but another shrewd New Yorker, also a product of the Thomas E. Dewey and Herbert Brownell schools, Tom Stephens. As Ann wrote to Hall, "He has been the most wonderful friend I could possibly have had, and has taught me a thousand and one political facts of life." To Adele Levy she wrote, "He's one of the truly rare people in the world."

Without question, Stephens was also one of the funniest persons who has ever worked in the White House. For many who were familiar with the scene then, memories of Tom Stephens's pranks and whimsicalities are as much a part of the Eisenhower administration as the programs and pronouncements now weighing down the shelves of the library in Abilene. Predictably, he was born in County Dublin, Ireland, and came to the United States with his parents as a child. His schooling was sporadic, but after a migratory career as a worker in a rubber-boot factory and as a raincoat salesman, ashtray manufacturer, and fraud investigator, he entered Republican politics in Manhattan while studying law at night at Brooklyn Law School. He was an inveterate collector. When he had a law office in New York, the items in it included bear traps, Geiger counters, rainfall-measuring kits, solar cookers from India, bits of the old Third Avenue "El," and portions of a consignment of camel saddles from Egypt. "There's going to be a big demand for camel saddles in this country some day," he said, "and I'll make a million dollars because I'll be the only one ready to supply the demand."

When Eisenhower returned in 1952 to run for president, Governor Dewey turned over to him some of the ablest members of his own staff, notably Stephens and Hagerty. In his memoirs Eisenhower called Stephens one of his ablest political advisers.

In Washington, Ann and Stephens lived in adjacent apartment houses on Massachusetts Avenue, near Sixteenth Street. In the morning they used to meet midway and make the twenty-minute walk down Sixteenth Street to the White House together. The walk took them past the old Soviet Embassy on the east side of Sixteenth Street, where they came to notice the gardener who worked on the grounds behind a high iron fence. Against Ann's wishes, Stephens began saying "Good morning" to the man, and in time the latter responded. After this ritual one day, the irrepressible Stephens suddenly doubled back and shouted to the gardener, "Thanks very much for the letter." Neither Stephens nor Ann ever knew why, but after another two weeks had passed, they never saw the man again.

Ann Whitman in her office at the Newport, Rhode Island, naval base where President Eisenhower vacationed in 1958.

(ABOVE) *Eisenhower and Ann in a light moment while he was vacationing in California during the first year of his retirement.* (BELOW) *Taking dictation in the Oval Office, June 1957.*

(PHOTO BY DOROTHY WILDING. COURTESY MRS. M^cX ASCOLI)

(ABOVE) *Adele Rosenwald Levy, an admired friend for whom Ann worked for sixteen years before going to the White House.*
(BELOW) *Mary Caffrey Stephens, secretary to White House Press Secretary James C. Hagerty and Ann's closest colleague.*

(ABOVE) *President Eisenhower with Thomas E. Stephens, his appointments secretary, and Ann at Palm Springs in February 1954.*

(OPPOSITE, TOP) *Ann with Sigurd Larmon aboard the Eisenhower campaign train in 1952. Larmon was president of the New York advertising firm of Young and Rubicam.*

(RIGHT) *The men in Ann's career: Nelson A. Rockefeller and Dwight D. Eisenhower. The photograph was taken in the White House when Rockefeller was sworn in as special assistant to the president.*

(RIGHT) *A scene familiar at airports around the world in 1953–61: Eisenhower, accompanied by his Air Force aide and pilot, Colonel William Draper, arriving for a conference or visit; Ann bringing up the rear with an armful of documents. White House Press Secretary James C. Hagerty holding his hat in the wind is at right.*

(NATIONAL PARK SERVICE PHOTO COURTESY DWIGHT D. EISENHOWER LIBRARY)

(OPPOSITE, BOTTOM) *With the assistance of Ann and his special counsel, Gerald D. Morgan, the president signs bills at his Gettysburg farm on August 9, 1955.*

(BELOW) *A gathering at Denver during one of the worst ordeals of Ann's career—Eisenhower's heart attack in September 1955. Left to right: Sherman Adams, assistant to the president; Vice President Richard M. Nixon; Dr. Paul Dudley White, Boston heart specialist; and Colonel (later General) John S. D. Eisenhower, the president's son.*

(RIGHT) *Ann and Mamie Eisenhower flanking a friend aboard the presidential yacht* Barbara Anne *in Newport, Rhode Island, in 1947.*

(BELOW) *A day at the Rockefeller estate in Pocantico Hills in Westchester, New York. Nelson A. Rockefeller with Mary Caffrey Stephens, Ann, and Thomas E. Stephens.*

(COURTESY THOMAS E. STEPHENS)

7

By early 1955 Ann had been President Eisenhower's secretary for two years. Her brown hair was graying, but her constitution had been thoroughly tested and proved suitable for the covered wagon. Hours were long and tiring. Working in the cockpit of the White House strained her mood at times, as it does nearly everyone's who attempts it. In one letter to Adele Levy, the period of which is uncertain because the letter was undated, Ann seemed distraught.

"These last weeks here," she wrote, "are simply awful: pressures, tempers, backing and filling, and lots of disillusionments. The Boss takes it as well as a human can, but a lot of us are on the ragged edge."

Years later she seemed puzzled in rereading this and some other plaintive letters. "I never enjoyed anything more than that job," she said. "It was important. Something new was happening all the time. A new gift. A new letter. A new idea. Headlines every day, and you were right there where it was all happening."

Her relationship with the president continued to be solid and affectionate. She especially liked work when Eisenhower vacationed in summers in Denver, because, as she put it, he wore sports clothes and was more relaxed and life around the office was less formal. On June 10, 1953, the day before her first birthday in the White House (her forty-fifth), he sent her a handwritten note, regretting that he would not be there the next day. "I'm sorry," he said, "to miss the opportunity—you are the most important person in the life of this office." When, a year later, on June 11, 1954, he returned from lunch, he handed her a twenty-dollar gold piece minted in 1890, the year of his birth. If he was in the habit of giving such gifts to others, it is not remembered.

The two years with the president had also been two years in which Ann struggled to maintain a marriage with a husband who lived and worked in New York and traveled extensively as part of his job. By the time the 1952 election was over and Ann found Eisenhower's offer irresistible, she had sensed certain strains in her twelve-year marriage. While, for example, she retained liberal convictions, Whit, as she perceived it, was turning increasingly toward what became known as Goldwater Republicanism, especially on the issue of labor's rights. Moreover, during a trip the two of them had taken to Central America in 1948, they had met an intelligent and attractive younger woman, Sigrid Taillon, whose father also worked for United Fruit. Later Sigrid returned to the United States, and Whit would see her. Their friendship continued after Ann moved to Washington. Despite Adele Levy's words of caution to her in the fall of 1952, however, Ann did not regard her marriage as seriously threatened. During her years in the White House, Whit frequently spent weekends in Washington and sometimes in Denver and Augusta, and she visited New York as often as possible. For years they had had a twelfth-floor apartment with two bedrooms and a small terrace at 230 East Seventy-third Street, which she loved.

"Whit is wonderful," Ann wrote to Adele in the fall of 1953. "Did you know he came out to Denver with me and had the time of his life (including winning some six hundred dollars at the races the first day he was there)?"

Whit made plans to spend Christmas of 1953 in Augusta. "I can't visualize what fun it will be for him," Ann confided to her friend. "I'll have to work like the devil and Augusta is far from the most pleasant town in the world. But, he may be able to get into some trouble with some of the newspaper people." Her forecast was close to the mark. Ann wrote to Adele:

January 1, 1954

Whit was here for an unhappy couple of days. He came down Christmas Eve, and we didn't arrive until around three the next afternoon, after a dreary Christmas lunch at Fort Benning. I worked the next couple of days—Saturday and Sunday from the usual eight in the morning until around six in the evening. At which time Whit took off from Augusta, shaking off the red clay and saying never again. I talked to him last night, both of us feeling fairly sorry for ourselves— he not knowing whether to go out on the town, and I to go to bed with a couple of sleeping pills at 9:30. All this sounds very dreary and believe me, it is.

Nevertheless, Whit braved Augusta again for another week-end at Christmas of 1954. The results were not much happier. Ann wrote:

Whit came down Friday and goes back to New York today; he has been stalwart but lonely, since we work all the time. He thought this morning he would go out to the airport to watch the [White House courier] plane come in—it's that bad!

If any emotional suffering was involved, Ann was character-istically tough and determined not to let it interfere with work.

The Whitmans' weekend visits, whether in Augusta or Washington, continued to be plagued by the problem of Ann's having to work long hours. When that was the case in the capital, Whit would sometimes head for southern Maryland where Tom Stephens had a farm, free of trespassers because of signs he had posted warning BEWARE OF SNAKES.

*   *   *

The year 1955 was an extraordinary one for Ann. Along with the very large events that involved her were certain smaller matters that caused no public notice. One of these was a personal letter she wrote on March 10 to James C. Stahlman, president of the *Nashville Banner*, protesting a recent editorial, which sternly but groundlessly accused Tom Stephens, as appointments secretary, of having refused to schedule Eisenhower for a dinner honoring former President Herbert Hoover. In fact, it was a staff decision of which Eisenhower had been fully aware. His schedule at the time was rigid, and Hoover himself urged him not to go to the dinner. In her letter explaining this to Stahlman, Ann wrote as good a definition of the difficulties and responsibilities of the White House staff as can be found anywhere.

> First of all—the White House staff is a human organization composed of men and women, who do get tired; who do lose their tempers; who do occasionally rub people against the grain; who sometimes, because an instant decision is required, may have to make up their minds before they have all the facts.
>
> Of course, in all their relations with the public, they must do everything they can to further the purposes of any person or group honestly and intelligently concerned with the betterment of the country. But the staff's first objective must always be such service to the President that he may most easily and wisely make decisions for himself. His peace of mind, for instance, must come first before the maintenance of the staff's own friendly relations with any individual or organization. That is true, too, of his schedule, the conservation of his energy, and scores of other factors that may affect his effectiveness.

She concluded with a paragraph that reads as if, consciously or otherwise, it was meant to apply to her as well as to her colleagues.

> A lawyer, writing of the White House staff, in a letter to a staff member today, said: "They slave as though they were going to get something tangible out of it; then, alas, they get only satisfaction with no time to enjoy it."

Ann had never been to Europe. In the summer of 1955 she went in style. In a decision that attracted the approving attention of the entire world, Eisenhower agreed to participate in a summit meeting in Geneva in July with Anthony Eden, who had succeeded Churchill as prime minister; Premier Edgar Faure of France, and the paired Soviet leaders, Nikita S. Khrushchev, head of the Communist party, and Premier Nicolai A. Bulganin.

"I think I ought to be beside myself with excitement at the approaching Geneva trip," Ann wrote to Adele on July 14, 1955. "Actually I seem to get calmer as the tensions mount."

Ann was aware how eagerly Churchill had sought a summit meeting before he left office, and she left a note about it on the president's desk.

July 14, 1955

None-of-my business again

If I were an old man who had dreamed of and worked hard and unsuccessfully for a Summit meeting for years, I would want more than anything a message from "my boy" as he approaches such a meeting.

I know it's sentimental, and I don't understand why Churchill did not respond to those two final letters from you, and I know you can't say anything that would hurt Eden's prestige—but

Eisenhower did not respond to the suggestion, possibly because he did not have enough time before departing.

Partly because he performed very well and partly because of the goodwill it engendered, the summit was one of the important events of Eisenhower's presidency. Substantively, the conference was more or less on a par with other postwar meetings among leaders of the East and West, before and since; in other words, it was unable to bridge the gap between the two sides in the Cold War. On the other hand, Eisenhower won a good deal of fame out of it, and Ann, who had a fairly easy few days, was delighted for him, as well as being fascinated by her Swiss surroundings. The sessions were held in the Palais des Nations, where she had an office adjoining the president's. While Eisenhower was domiciled in a villa—the same one that President Ronald Reagan occupied during his meeting with Mikhail Gorbachev in 1985—Ann stayed in the Hotel du Rhone. She liked it especially because the sound of the nearby rushing river made sleeping a delight. In a letter to Helen Weaver, a colleague at the White House, she described the hotel as "de luxe and gadget-y beyond anything I have seen. The food of course is superb."

During the day Ann divided her time between the hotel and the Palais, where "the telephones strictly don't work." She was forever "running around to be within call should the President want anything; and with characteristic fashion, [I] was not around almost the one time he did want anything. Life is simple, since all the mail, or almost all, has to go to State (being in a foreign language)."

She wrote to Whit, who was planning to join her later in the summer in Denver:

> I miss you and wish you were here; but there would be no time to enjoy this really lovely spot. I'd like to explore a little alley that seemed full of antique shops (we had dinner in it one night late); I'd like to walk around and look at the shops.

Beyond quaintness, Ann found Geneva and the gathering of national leaders exciting. "The moment that gave me the greatest pause," she wrote to Whit, "was when I picked up the phone and was informed that Marshal Zhukov wanted to speak to the President on the phone.* My question to the voice at the other end, which spoke passable English, was, I think, pertinent—'But how can he?' Through an interpreter it was arranged." In her office in the Palais there was a space of a few inches under the door to the corridor. Glancing through the space from her desk, she could differentiate among certain of the delegations who walked past because the cuffs of the trousers of

* Marshal Georgi K. Zhukov, who had commanded the central front against the Germans and later became Soviet minister of defense, had fallen from power by the time of the summit meeting.

the Western delegates were neatly tailored, whereas the shape of those worn by the Soviets was almost bell bottom. "Bulganin looks exactly like Santa Claus in the flesh," she wrote to Adele Levy, "and Marshal Zhukov was just as resplendent as it is possible for a human to be." Draped with medals, Ann recalled afterward, the marshal was spectacular when he called on Eisenhower in an open car that took two steps to mount. "I later suggested to the president," she confided to Adele, "that he get done up in uniform and all the medals and outshine him—but my special brand of diplomacy was ignored."

The climax of the Geneva Conference was Eisenhower's speech proposing his open-skies plan. It would have granted to signatory powers the right to conduct aerial photography over one anothers' territories as assurance against preparations for surprise attack. The Soviets were no more interested in it than they had been nearly two years earlier in the atoms-for-peace program. When the conference adjourned, Ann recalled, Eisenhower sat at the desk in his office, disappointed with the results. Suddenly he summoned her and either Charles E. Bohlen or Llewellyn E. Thompson—Ann could not recall which; both of those leading American experts on the Soviet Union attended the conference. With Ann and whichever of the two men it was, the president set off along the corridor of Bulganin's office to see the premier. "He just didn't want the summit to end in discouragement," she said. "I think he simply intended to ask Bulganin to join us for a drink." The premier, however, had already left the Palais.

"It disturbs me," she commented thirty-four years later, "when anyone compares President Reagan and President Eisenhower [in respect to Soviet-American relations]. President Reagan is such a hard-liner. President Eisenhower disliked and disapproved of Communism, but he had faith in friendship and peace. He really thought the nations of the world could be friends, that programs to bring people together had a chance. His instinct was to reach out."

The trip back to Washington had a hilarious ending, even though to Ann it seemed a personal calamity.

The propeller-driven *Columbine II* stopped at Bangor, Maine, for refueling. By then the passengers had been in their berths for about twelve hours and were restless. Ann suggested to some of her colleagues that they join her in a walk around the base. From the pilot, Colonel Draper, they obtained an estimate of the refueling time and set off, knowing exactly when to return. The refueling operation, however, was a much shorter one than Draper had calculated, and some passengers had to be sent out in search of Ann and her companions. Painfully aware that *nobody* keeps the president waiting, Ann, completely crestfallen, finally scrambled back aboard. Eisenhower "growled at me that he had told the pilot to take off without us," she said. Worse was yet to come. Much worse. Because of the delay in takeoff at Bangor, the plane landed seven minutes late at Washington National Airport. And as a result of Ann's walk and one of Vice-President Nixon's unbearably clever inspirations, the ceremony before a large crowd of welcomers was a disaster. The seven lost minutes had provided time for a downpour to sweep across the airport, and the government officials who dominated the crowd had no umbrellas. Outdoing himself as an impresario, Nixon had given orders that no umbrellas were to be carried lest they recall the very symbol of British Prime Minister Neville Chamberlain's ill-fated return to London from the Munich Conference in 1938. For whatever reason, the president did not carry an umbrella either, and he got soaked along with everyone else.

"I am still getting snide remarks about it from Bill Draper," Ann wrote two weeks later. "It was not a happy ending to a trip that was for me sheer wonderment."

When things settled down, however, she was pleased to get a letter from as loyal a Democrat as Adele Levy, saying how impressed she had been with Eisenhower's performance in Geneva. Ann replied, elatedly:

August 6, 1955

Of course you know that nothing could please me more than to have *you* say that you are proud of the President's performance. . . . It was truly magnificent, and would have been even more brilliant if he had not been held down by State Department stuffiness. No one, even a Russian, can hold out against his sincerity and his unaffected and totally spontaneous charm. Call it his Kansas-boy approach if you will, and some do, but it is refreshing. . . . I respect and honor you so much and the President so much too, that I ran in to him with your note, and I think he was as delighted as I was.

New diversions were in store for Ann as Eisenhower prepared to leave for his vacation in Denver. Still, she expected it to be less fun for her than before. "This year," she wrote to Adele, "I sadly predict a quiet and dull time out there because my special friends—Tom Stephens and Merriman Smith—are not going to be with the party, but the mountains and sunsets and lots of things I love will still be around."

What with Geneva behind him, with the dangers of imminent military involvement in Indochina and the Formosa Straits reduced, and McCarthy defanged by censure, Eisenhower was enjoying perhaps the quietest interlude any president has known since that day. The prospect of tranquil weeks was so convincing that Sherman Adams and his wife were on a European tour, along with Goodpaster. Jim Hagerty was vacationing at home in Washington, leaving the presidential press headquarters in Denver in the hands of his assistant, Murray Snyder, a former political writer for the *New York Herald Tribune*. Ann, of course, was on the job as usual in an office adjoining the president's at Lowry Air Force Base at Denver. She was not staying at one of her favorite hotels, the Brown Palace. The daily travel allowance for government employees put it beyond the reach of Ann and the rest of the staff. They lived in air force quarters at Lowry—"barracks," Ann called them. "Ah, but in Denver," she wrote again to Mrs. Levy, "I have a car (usually a pink and purple convertible) and every morning I get up at my usually indecent hour and drive toward the mountains."

Her work was relatively easy because Eisenhower spent a good deal of time golfing at the Cherry Hill Country Club. He and Ann had some relaxed talks. It was another unusual bit of evidence of the candor of their relationship that he had once instructed her to watch him carefully for any sign of physical deterioration. Having entered the White House at sixty-two, which was considered older then than it is now, he seems to have been keenly aware of the potential problem of aging for a president. It is hard to imagine any other recent president we have known instructing his personal secretary to be on the lookout for any sign that he was growing old, slowing down, or manifesting an impairment.

Certainly, Ann saw nothing about his health to disturb her in Denver, as August turned to September and the president went on relishing fishing, cooking outdoors, and playing golf. On the morning of September 23, he returned in good spirits from four days at his friend Aksel Nielsen's Byers Peak Ranch in Fraser, Colorado. When he arrived at his office at Lowry, Ann thought she had never seen him look or act better. She noted in her diary:

> *He was delightful, patient with the pile of work, handed me a letter from Dr. Milton and said, "See what a wonderful brother I have." He sat and talked for a little while after he got through work before he went to the golf course. On the way out I screamed after him (George Allen was waiting downstairs in the car), "Tell Mr. Allen I shan't forgive him for not coming up to see me." He did so the minute he got in the car.*

After his golf game Eisenhower returned to the unpretentious eight-room gray brick house of Mrs. John S. Doud, his mother-in-law, at 750 Lafayette Street, where he and Mamie were staying. It was four miles from Lowry.

Ann, after an uneventful day, turned in, as usual, in her quarters at the base and went to sleep. The next day, which was a Saturday and thus expected to be especially restful, she was awakened by the ring of the telephone next to her bed. It was 6:45 A.M. One of her warm friends on the White House staff, Major General Howard McC. Snyder, was calling. A tall, erect, white-haired, bespectacled, delightful man, he had earned Ann's accolade of "old duck." At seventy-four, he was personal physician to President Eisenhower, as he had been in Europe to

General Eisenhower. Snyder told Ann that the president would not be in early that morning, but might show up at 10 o'clock or so—a peculiar thing to tell her, as matters stood. Then he passed on some instructions.

When reporters began arriving at Lowry in a couple of hours and found that Eisenhower was not there, they would surely question Murray Snyder (no relation) regarding his whereabouts. General Snyder told Ann that Murray was to say that the president was troubled by a "digestive upset." This information caused Ann no qualms, because Eisenhower had a history of upset stomach.

After breakfast she went to her office. At around 11 o'clock, Robert E. Clark, the White House correspondent for the old International News Service, called from the Lowry pressroom. He said that because Murray Snyder was reluctant to declare that Eisenhower's "digestive upset" was not serious—how could he when he did not know the extent of the problem?—the wire services were blowing Eisenhower's condition "up into some major illness." Clark asked Ann to call General Snyder and ask him to inform Murray whether the president's condition was or was not serious. Ann set to work on Clark's request, and after about forty-five minutes General Snyder sent word that the president's "digestive upset" was not serious. This statement was carried on the wire services and published in the afternoon newspapers. Doubly reassured, Ann, Murray Snyder, Betty Allen, a secretary in the press office, and Ann Parsons, a secretary to Mrs. Eisenhower, took a couple of White House cars to go to lunch at a restaurant called the Famous Chef.

That they should have been left for so long in ignorance of what was happening is astonishing. After returning from golf Friday evening, Eisenhower did not feel well. He went to sleep but awoke at 1:30 A.M. with a severe chest pain. Mrs. Eisenhower telephoned General Snyder. Within minutes of his arrival Snyder concluded that the president was suffering from a coronary thrombosis, although he could not assess the extent of damage to the heart.

The episode is unmatched in American history. The president was lying in a room in a house in Denver in the middle of the night with a heart attack. Only one person in the world, Howard Snyder, knew it, as he informed neither the president nor Mrs. Eisenhower of his tentative diagnosis. No oxygen supply was available. He did not summon an ambulance. Snyder was not a heart specialist. No second opinion was immediately sought, no consultation arranged. Snyder later told Ann, as she recorded the conversation in her diary, that it was "better to let the president sleep and his system get over the initial shock, rather than to wake him and get him to a hospital immediately."

The United States and the Soviet Union were armed with nuclear weapons. By law, the American weapons could be used only on the authority of the president. The president was about to be sedated by his physician. Unaware of the drama in Denver, the vice-president was asleep at his home in Washington. No one notified the secretary of state or the secretary of defense. Up to that time no procedures had been adopted for the temporary transfer of power to the vice-president in case the president was incapacitated.

With Eisenhower now in a deep sleep, Snyder passed the night with him, knowing a secret that would have shocked the world. In the wake of Geneva, Eisenhower's prestige abroad and popularity at home were unparalleled. The foundations of such détente as the world has known since 1945 were largely the result of his continuing efforts. No other American, certainly not Nixon at that time, could have dealt with the Soviet leaders on anything near as reasonable a basis as Eisenhower. And the death or disability of General Snyder's patient would have blown into political turmoil an America in the most tranquil state it had known in thirty years. In the aftershocks of McCarthyism, millions of Democrats loathed and feared Nixon for his red-baiting and sympathy for McCarthy. His sudden elevation to the presidency would have turned the 1956 election into an indescribably bitter fight. Wall Street and the conservatives would have had some reason to fear that instead of four more years of Eisenhower, beginning

January 20, 1957, a successor regime to the New Deal and the Fair Deal might be back in power in Washington.

The reasons why Howard Snyder, a man of native good sense, acted in such an unacceptable way in concealing the president's condition seem rather obvious. As a general and a physician, he was conservative, not one to want to set off fireworks in every newsroom on earth. He undoubtedly sought, for the president's own good, to protect Eisenhower from excitement. Snyder knew that concealment would deflect a rush of reporters and photographers to the front door. He had long been very close to the Eisenhower family and surely hoped to keep Mrs. Eisenhower from being overly upset. If Hagerty, who had far more authority than Murray Snyder, had been in Denver, he surely would have intervened the moment he heard about the "digestive upset." Unquestionably, he would have found a way promptly to inform the press of the seriousness of the president's condition, while having the Doud house cordoned off to protect the president from clamor. Around noon on Saturday, the president rode in his own limousine to Fitzsimmons Army Hospital in Denver, there to learn the nature of his illness.

At the Famous Chef, Ann and her colleagues were waiting for their lunch to be served when, at one forty-five, Murray Snyder was called to the telephone. What followed, Ann remembers to this day as a nightmare. Snyder darted back to the table, told the three women that the president had suffered a "mild anterior coronary thrombosis," and then rushed to Lowry in one of the two cars. Ann and her two other friends paid the bill for an unserved lunch and hastened after him in the other car.

Ann's office was a maelstrom. She had scarcely settled at the desk when General Snyder called. She noted in her diary that Snyder told her the president's eyes filled with tears when they placed him in an oxygen tent, and added, "Of course he knew it was serious—he mentioned his wallet to General Snyder and some money I have for him." The purpose of Snyder's call was to pass on instructions to her from Eisenhower. He wanted her to call Attorney General Brownell and have him prepare an opinion on how the president could delegate authority when he was ill. Unable to locate Brownell, she called Deputy Attorney General William P. Rogers, Jr., and he set to work on the subject.

All afternoon and late into the night Ann was on the telephone almost continuously, with sometimes six calls stacked up with the base operators. She called Nixon and the secretaries of state and defense and then Secretary of the Interior Weeks and Postmaster General Arthur E. Summerfield. She talked with Bernard M. Shanley, then special counsel to the president, who was in Tokyo. She telephoned each of the Eisenhower brothers, beginning with Milton. Because it was a Saturday afternoon, she had difficulty reaching the president's personal friends, but managed to get in touch with Ellis D. Slater, president of the Frankfurt Distillers Corporation, William E. Robinson, then-publisher of the *Herald Tribune*, and Clifford Roberts, a prominent stockbroker.

"It was Mr. Roberts," she wrote in her diary, "who insisted and arranged for a civilian doctor, Dr. Paul Dudley White, to come out from Boston on Sunday. His reasoning was that while the army doctors were no doubt competent, we would be criticized for not bringing in civilian consultants. . . ."

Hagerty, whom Murray Snyder had immediately notified of the president's condition, got through to Ann on the telephone. She burst out crying. "Please hurry and get out here as soon as you can," she pleaded. "Both General Snyder and I need you." Ann had been calling Walter Reed Hospital in Washington to ask that Colonel Thomas W. Mattingly be found and flown to Denver at once. He was the physician who had conducted all Eisenhower's physical examinations after he became president and was most familiar with Eisenhower's recent normal health patterns. He and Hagerty flew to Denver on the same plane.

For at least forty-eight hours the White House offices at Lowry were in bedlam. Russell Baker, *The New York Times* reporter on the scene, wrote that "the summer White House has changed from a scene of golden, indolent tranquility to a cold, gray, chaotic nightmare." Messages flooded in from Queen Elizabeth II, Prime Minister Jawaharlal Nehru of India, General Charles de Gaulle, Chancellor Konrad Adenauer of West Germany, Generalissimo Chiang Kai-shek of Nationalist China, Bulganin, Churchill, and Senator Lyndon B. Johnson of Texas, who had suffered a heart attack the previous July. The two living former presidents, Herbert Hoover and Harry Truman, voiced dismay. On Sunday, at his summer residence at Castel Gandolfo in Italy, Pope Pius XII prayed for Eisenhower's recovery. Clifton Daniel reported in *The New York Times* that worshipers wept in Moscow's Baptist Church. In the United States, prayers for the president were offered everywhere, including all eight masses in St. Patrick's Cathedral in New York. Leading columnists were already speculating that Eisenhower would not run for reelection in 1956. On Monday, September 26, the stock market suffered its worst dollar loss in history up to that time. The value of shares on the New York Stock Exchange fell by $14 billion—though a trivial sum compared with the $500 billion loss on "Black Monday," October 19, 1987.

When the weekend had passed, Ann noted in her diary:

Sunday is already a daze—mostly telephoning. Monday morning was the first sign of good news, and each morning thereafter it has been better. When the president woke up and said, "Where's my breakfast?" I cried. When it was reported to me that he asked about me, I cried. The first three days I was strong enough—then I collapsed and still am.

When Ann first saw Eisenhower after the attack, he was still in an oxygen tent. Although he progressed remarkably well, his recovery required a stay of nearly seven weeks at Fitzsimmons. Adams had returned from Europe immediately and at the end of September took over an office at Lowry. The president's steady improvement ended talk about delegation of authority. With Congress in adjournment and foreign affairs unusually quiet, no strain was placed upon him. He eased his way back into discharge of his duties throughout October with a series of leisurely conferences at his bedside with Adams and Ann, who took notes. The items of business were relatively minor and, as Ann's diary reveals, gave Eisenhower a chance to philosophize about people and things.

> *October 10, 1955*
> *President mentioned Nixon's visit and said that his illness, he thought, had turned public attention pretty sharply toward Nixon. "He is a darn good young man." Adams said that the necessity for making decisions, the lack of having the President to lean on, was making all Administration people "sharpen their wits."*

Eisenhower ruminated on whether the doctrine that a man's home is his castle applies in the case of a farm where the farmer abused the soil—"was permitted to ruin it." A nation, he told Ann and Adams, "cannot divest itself of interest in its own soil." The president also talked about a difficult situation that had existed between Dulles and Nelson Rockefeller before Rockefeller's recent resignation as special assistant to the president for psychological warfare. Dulles grumbled that Rockefeller was intruding on the secretary of state's domain. "Here is one place where the President thinks the Secretary of State may have been hyper-sensitive," Ann noted. "President said, 'Give me a gadfly now and again—give me someone who will make certain things are not forgotten.' Again he said, 'I am astonished at the sensitivity of big people' to what they consider encroachment in their field. They are afraid prestige will be lost." Adams asked Eisenhower if he would like to have the speechwriter Kevin McCann and General Persons come to Denver to give him an idea how the 1956 State of the Union message was shaping up.*

"President," Ann jotted, "would like some idea of 'tone'— but said he found when a new idea was presented he got enthusiastic about it at first, but soon lost interest in it."

* General Wilton B. Persons was then the deputy assistant to the president in charge of legislative liaison.

Eisenhower was more concerned about how well he could discharge his presidential duties than about his own fate, as Ann noted.

October 26, 1955
[The president] said that the doctors tell him that almost four months from the day of his illness they will take all sorts of tests and can predict to a certainty how much of his previous activity he can renew. He said, "For myself I don't much care, I have had a pretty good life. I am not too much concerned with me."

Answering the wave of mail Eisenhower received on his sixty-fifth birthday in the hospital on October 14 "almost did me under," Ann wrote to Adele Levy. But birthday greetings were only part of the problem. Some newspaper columnist multiplied her labors by writing that the president wanted, as she said to Adele, "to hear about all the babies born on his sixty-fifth birthday." Ann informed her friend:

Now all the proud parents are writing in and [asking] for a little something to give the baby as he grows older. I grew grayer with that one.
But my favorite of the day is the lady from Minnesota who wrote the President saying "I would like to have a personal statement from you to this, 'Have you had a personal experience with the Lord? Are you a 'born again Christian?' " That one I think I shall have filed without answer.

On Eisenhower's behalf, Ann sent a note of inquiry to Adams that, if it had become public, would have brought howls of glee from Dulles's critics, especially those who charged that "pactomania" ruled his diplomacy.

November 2, 1955

Governor Adams:

President asks if the Baghdad Pact the same as the Northern Tier Pact?

a.

The correct answer to the question was yes.* To the critics the query would have been the ultimate proof that Dulles had encouraged the formation of so many anti-Soviet alliances around the world that even the president could not keep track of them.

Ann helped keep the stable as Eisenhower convalesced.

November 8, 1955

Governor Adams:

Eventually the President should, I suspect, answer this letter from Earl Mountbatten. I showed it to him this afternoon, and he made some comment to the effect that it was very short-sighted of the American government not to cooperate fully with the British in the matter of building an atomic submarine. Is there any way in which the Attorney General could be asked to rule on the matter of giving them information, without too much delay?

Ann

Eisenhower was due to be discharged from the hospital on November 11. In the days before that date, Ann sometimes accompanied him to a nearby stairwell to watch him practice climbing fourteen steps to convince himself that he could surely make it up the ramp to his plane. With full television coverage at both ends, the journey back to Washington was something of a day of national rejoicing.

For Christmas, Eisenhower gave Ann book No. 42 in a special limited edition of 1,426 copies of his *Crusade in Europe*, which he inscribed:

For Ann Whitman

The world's finest secretary!
With deep and lasting appreciation of her skilled and devoted services since the summer of 1952; and with affectionate regard from her friend

Merry Christmas 1955
Dwight D. Eisenhower

---

* Signed the previous February 24, Dulles had helped to bring the treaty into being, but at first the pact was restricted to Turkey, Iran, Iraq, Pakistan, and Great Britain. Later it was transformed into the Central Treaty Organization, supported but not joined by the United States.

Then on New Year's Eve he wrote in longhand the following letter:

DDE

Dec. 31, '55.
The White House

Dear Ann—

I wish I knew how to thank you for all you have done to make my life and my work easier during the year just past. Your competence in your importance [sic] post is matched only by the complete devotion you give to it. I earnestly hope you realize that I am grateful.

But if I do not have the words to tell you how deeply obligated to you I feel—I can at least say "Happy New Year." May 1956 be the best year of your life, so far! In these sentiments Mrs. Eisenhower joins me, as well as in the warmest good wishes and regard to you.

Sincerely D.E.

Mrs. Ann Whitman
Confidential, Personal Secretary

8

After the crisis in Denver and the weeks of working quietly with the president in his hospital room during convalescence, Ann's role was more assured than ever. Eisenhower's New Year's letter only reinforced the observations of others about his reliance on her. However gratifying this must have been to her on the one hand, on the other it insured a continuing and, if anything, heavier load of work with long hours and little time off.

One evening around six-thirty a few months after their return from Denver Ann and her colleague Helen Weaver, a WAVE who had been Eisenhower's secretary at NATO, were nearing what they hoped was the end of a hard day. Then Eisenhower said to them, "Well, I must go home so you girls can go back to work." It was a Saturday. "There never was a truer statement," Ann told Adele Levy in recounting the incident, "than the Presidency is a twenty-four-hour-a-day job because there are certain things that have to go to him at any hour, [at the] swimming pool, or late at night at home."

In his biography of Eisenhower, Professor Ambrose wrote that the president drove Ann like a slave from dawn to dusk. "At times, yes," she agreed in retrospect, "but he wasn't conscious of it. He did not drive me. I assumed all the work." "I have a strong constitution," she commented on another occasion. "I could go without sleep, live on peppermint patties and sandwiches. I don't think President Eisenhower knew how hard I worked." Indeed there is little doubt Ann worked harder than she had to, strictly speaking. It was a characteristic of hers, wherever she worked, to take a proprietary interest in her job. She and nobody else was going to do what needed to be done. There was no regulation that she had to work by herself in the White House on Saturday afternoons and Sundays to double-check presidential correspondence, for instance. During the week as a general rule she worked late in the evening, went out to dinner with some other woman on the staff, returned to her apartment and read or watched television, and went to sleep. It was often much the same on trips. On the forthcoming visit to India, when nearly everyone else took leave of New Delhi one Saturday and went to visit the Taj Mahal in Agra, Ann stayed at her desk to type a speech text and turn out letters thanking Indian donors for gifts to the president. As always, he wanted such letters sent before departing.

That Eisenhower took it for granted that he would be waited on by secretaries, aides-de-camp, valets, butlers, caddies, doctors, and others was so obvious as to be commonplace. One day his casual expectation of personal services was a topic of discussion between two friends of his and of Ann's. One was Jacqueline Cochran, an outstanding aviator, and the other was Freeman Gosden, a golfing partner of the president's. Gosden had been the Amos of the famous radio program "Amos and Andy" and sometimes lapsed into the dialect, to the amusement of Ann and others. Cochran quoted Gosden as having asked during their discussion, "I wonder if General Eisenhower ever realized the number of people that just surrounded him with love and care and attention, where he never had any problems whatsoever of any description?"

In Washington, Ann severely subordinated social life to work, a custom she later somewhat regretted. Embassy parties are not the Yale proms of lore, but they are a part of the official life of the capital. Personal enjoyment is not absolutely proscribed. In eight years Ann went to one of them—not to eat strawberries and cream in the gardens of the British Embassy but to accompany Tom Stephens to an affair at the Embassy of the Dominican Republic. Sometimes she got away from the White House for lunch at the Hay-Adams Hotel or the old Occidental Restaurant on Pennsylvania Avenue. Mostly, however, she had her lunch brought to her office, where she and Stephens frequently ate together. On Ann's lucky days Jack Martin and Gerald Morgan would return early from lunch outside, with one of them miraculously carrying a martini in his pocket to place on her desk before her tray arrived.

Of course, members of the White House staff manage to have their own fun on occasion, especially when the president is on a reasonably relaxed trip. The Eisenhower administration was no exception. Nevertheless, Ann's job dragged her through some very weary times. That she liked it, was proud of it, and would not have changed it for any other does not alter the fact that heavy work and tiring schedules, especially on rushed trips, sometimes oppressed her. Even though she might not accept this in retrospect, her diary and contemporary letters clearly show the signs. On November 6, 1956, she wrote to Adele Levy:

> Actually, I do nothing—speaking of social things—at all. I work twelve hours a day, practically ten hours every Saturday and Sunday, and go to bed at nine every night. If I am lucky, I look at television for a half hour before sleep overtakes me. . . .

The saving factor was always her resilience. It was undoubtedly true that anyone who might have encountered her on the same day that she had written such a letter would have found her laughing and joking. To her friends, colleagues, and acquaintances Ann was much more interesting and vital than the tone of a spontaneous letter like this one might suggest. Partly it was because of her risibility; partly because of her warm personality with pockets of acerbity. Moreover, she had an appeal because of the very wide sympathy she manifested for the problems and troubles of others. On a different level she was a true insider, full of secrets, a player who could quietly put the dart in the bull's-eye of the president's opponents and in that of anyone else who displeased her. Yet when she was not terrifying the typing pool, she had the easy and pleasing style of an attractive middle-aged woman who had reached the heights. She was invariably interesting to talk to because she had a quick, natural curiosity about what someone else had to say.

Her hard work and long hours did not go unrecognized. William Hopkins who went to work in the White House in 1931 when Hoover was president and retired as chief clerk during the Nixon administration, had long been familiar with the performances of presidential secretaries. From the vantage point of 1985, he said that never in all his years had he seen anything to equal the volume and excellence of Ann's work.

To her, the worth of the job transcended its hardships. She was devoted to Eisenhower. She regarded him as a great man, a good man who tried to do what was right, even though in rare cases she might not agree with it. She considered it an honor to help him. She had won high standing in the White House and among hundreds of men and women on the outside who had dealings with the White House or with the president personally. She was convinced that the Eisenhower administration was doing things for the good of the nation and the world, and she felt she had her own small share in this history.

After Eisenhower's health had been restored and he returned to normal activities in 1956, a presidential election year, he paid a brief visit in February to Thomasville, a tidy and quiet town in the flat piney country of south-central Georgia. Secretary of the Treasury George M. Humphrey and Jock Whitney had plantations nearby, where Eisenhower enjoyed hunting quail. Ann was with him on the trip, of course, staying with the rest of the staff and the press at a modern hotel in town. An earlier trip to Thomasville had been impressed upon her memory as if by a demolition ball. In a letter to Marie McCrum, who was C. D. Jackson's secretary, Ann once described the terrors in landing that day in a violent storm.

> We went in finally with a ceiling of less than a hundred feet; no one saw the ground until we bumped on it—and I mean bumped; one of the girls next to me chose that moment to get violently sick; I jumped up instinctively and got thrown around madly, landing finally in General Snyder's lap (and with a noisy reprimand from the President), and one of the crew members slid the entire length of the plane, on his stomach.

The weather was pleasant enough for the February trip, taken at a time when politics was dominated by the question of whether Eisenhower would run again. He had still not declared. Ann and Mary Caffrey were riding together behind his car in Georgia on the drive from the airport. Crowds of schoolchildren were waiting at various crossroads to watch him pass. At each gathering he had his driver stop so he could wave. Simultaneously at one point Ann and Mary said to each other, "He's going to run!" In town Ann wrote to Adele Levy:

> Actually, the hotel is fine and the town not nearly as bad as some of the places we have "visited"—notably Gettysburg and Augusta. We are all so pious as to be unrecognizable, since there isn't a drink to be had in town; additionally a lot of my friends take Lent seriously and one or two of the others are on a health binge. It all adds up to lots of sleep and good books, which I am certain you approve. . . .
> Incidentally, I don't remember whether I have mentioned it before or not, probably I have, possibly the most rewarding part of this whole experience is the friendship I have made with the newspaper men. Without exception, they are intelligent, fun, alert— and I learn so much from them. At first we were unfortunately afraid of them, afraid to talk to them for fear we would say something that we would find in the paper the next day. Now they actually protect us— and despite their idiosyncrasies, which are many, a wonderful group of people whom I much admire and respect.

Eisenhower's decision to seek a second term was hardly surprising. On February 29, 1956, he dictated to Ann his statement that "my answer will be positive, that is affirmative." The next eight months were particularly hectic for his staff, what with the national conventions and the campaign, complicated by serious crises at Suez and in Hungary. "When this Mid East thing began," Ann informed Adele, "I had orders not to go more than 15 minutes away from a telephone, which rather precluded New York and other delightful things." One of the entries in her diary painted an unconsciously droll picture of a president not about to overtax himself.

June 4, 1956

Just before he left the office, he told me that he thought it would, or ought, to be possible to set down on paper what the foreign policy ought to be—he is thinking in terms of an actual chart that would be applicable in terms of all countries. He starts with the premise that Communism is an ideology that seeks to defeat us by every possible means. He went home determined to work on it, but reported next morning that instead he had gone to a movie.

The potentially hazardous issue of a president's campaigning for reelection soon after a heart attack was muted by Eisenhower's public display of energy and activity after his splendid recovery. On June 7, 1956, for example, he had arrived at his office at 7:57 A.M. His full day's schedule began in earnest with a two-hour meeting of the National Security Council. At 5:15 P.M., typically, he went out and hit golf balls on the South Lawn, this time with a friend, Clarence Schoo, president of the General Fibre Box Company of Springfield, Massachusetts. At six-fifty-five, the president departed for the annual dinner of the White House News Photographers Association at the Sheraton Park Hotel, returning after eleven o'clock. Then his schedule ran off the track. Again, in the dead of night, Howard Snyder received a call that the president was ill and rushed to the White House.

The next day, Friday, June 8, was eight months and fifteen days from the morning in Denver when Ann had received, at 6:45 A.M., the call from General Snyder saying that the president was suffering from a digestive upset and would not be in his office early. On this particular Friday morning, the call came one hour and five minutes later than that.

According to her diary:

> *At about 7:50 General Snyder called me from the President's bedroom saying that the President had a headache and digestive upset and that all appointments, save Cabinet, were to be cancelled. Cabinet was to be put at 2:00 P.M.*
>
> *I called Governor Adams, who said he would "take care of it." We notified most of Cabinet members.*

Hagerty, on the scene now as he had not been in Denver, went to the White House promptly. Ann was soon told, as she noted, that the president "was far sicker than had been thought." This time no concealment followed. Colonel Francis W. Pruitt of Walter Reed Hospital was called in around 11 A.M., and soon Eisenhower was taken to the hospital in an ambulance. He was suffering from a severe attack of ileitis, an intestinal inflammation that had troubled him on occasion in the past. Ann's diary traced the drama:

> *A bulletin issued around 8 in the evening indicated that probably surgery would not be necessary, but that the doctors (by this time a team of some 13 had been assembled) would re-examine the case at 12 midnight. The President's heart continued strong, giving no trouble at all—though Dr. White was called, or came, and Colonel Mattingly also returned quickly from his vacation.*
>
> *At 12:30 A.M. I was advised that probably there would be an operation; about 2:15 that there definitely would be. The operation began just before 3 and was concluded just before 5.*

General Snyder told Ann that when surgery was decided upon, the doctors first had the operating room readied and a stretcher waiting. Then at 2 A.M. they entered the president's room and informed him that in their collective opinion he should undergo an immediate operation. He said, in almost the same words he had used to order Allied forces to cross the English Channel and invade Normandy despite dangerously stormy weather, "Well, let's go."* When the anesthetic was being administered, Ann later learned, he said to General Leonard Heaton, commanding officer at Walter Reed and head of the team of surgeons: "You know, Leonard, I have a lot of bills to sign and I am going to have to be able to sign them within three or fours days. . . ." Then, Ann noted, "he added something about the Constitution . . . and went off." In contrast to Denver, too, when he was absent, General Goodpaster this time posted himself at the hospital, as he said, to "observe [the president's] competency should any military decisions become urgent."

A new wave of sympathy and concern over Eisenhower's health meant staggering work for Ann in answering letters and telegrams and acknowledging gifts. Lyndon Johnson, not to be outdone by anyone, sent Eisenhower flowers every day he was in Walter Reed. "I am literally on the ropes," Ann said in a joint letter to two New York friends, Marie Clancy and Madeline Earle. "Everything has to be answered, and everything has to be different." The rule also applied to telephone calls. As a consequence, Ann said, "I am in one of my I-hate-people moods." She was so angry at the resurgence of speculation as to whether Eisenhower would run that she loathed picking up newspapers or listening to broadcasts. She wrote in her letter:

> Things had been going along extremely well. . . . The President looked wonderfully, was extremely jovial and was taking everything in his stride. He had a terrible day before this occurred, but was in wonderful spirits even so. So I have no idea, nor has anyone explained to me, why it should have happened at this particular time. But it did. And I do think there is some bad management somewhere to give such a fine guy two bad times like this in something like [several] months.

She added:

> One thing, I have had experience in this line of work! . . . I live on dexamyl—and don't tell Mrs. Levy. We call them "jolly pills" and

---

* Launching the invasion, he was reported to have said, "Okay. We'll go."

they do wonderful things to you like making you able to do twice the work you normally could and that sort of thing. After about three in a day, then you have to take a sleeping pill to get some rest, but that is routine, too.

In periods of strenuous work that ruined much of the night for sleeping, especially on Eisenhower's long and often exhausting flights abroad, the White House medical staff under General Snyder freely dispensed Dexamyl and sleeping pills to members of the staff who felt a need for them. The pills were also dispensed to traveling reporters and photographers who wanted them.

Eisenhower's operation proved to be a cure, and he was soon back in good health, though doubts about his being able to run for a second term persisted.

Before the attack of ileitis he had accepted an invitation to visit Panama in the heat of July. With the operation behind him, he was determined to go, perhaps to make a point. Before taking off from Washington on July 20, he told General Persons, "If I don't feel better than this pretty soon, I'm going to pull out of this whole thing [the campaign]." Persons's subsequent account tells the story fairly well: "So he goes down to Panama, almost gets crushed by the mobs . . . suffers through all the damn receptions—and . . . three days later, he comes waltzing back looking like a new man." The trip was not that salubrious for a weary Ann Whitman. Having been under pressure for days and emotionally taut, she was seized by her I-hate-the-world or, as she sometimes described it, "malcontent" mood. She refused to return on the presidential plane, boarding the press plane instead. Her presence there aroused considerable curiosity because, before takeoff, the public address system on the plane kept paging her to return to her usual place. She would not budge. Eisenhower was indignant over her absence on the flight home. She apologized to him the next day, and the incident apparently was forgotten.

* * *

Eisenhower and Nixon were renominated to run against an ineffectual Democratic ticket of Adlai Stevenson and Senator Estes Kefauver of Tennessee. As in 1952, Eisenhower had overwhelming press support. Ann's diary cited an instance:

October 11, 1956

> He returned [from a luncheon] in time to read an editorial from Scripps-Howard chain saying "We Still Like Ike"—just before he saw the Prince and Princess of Monaco. Later the President said that the former Grace Kelly was aloof, but that the Prince was nice. The President gave the Prince a cigarette lighter, nothing to Miss Kelly. They both gave the President and Mrs. Eisenhower the medallion prepared for their wedding.

Politics obviously was not Eisenhower's only interest that fall. On October 30, for example, Ann found him in relaxed good humor. "He spent all the moments he had free," she noted in her diary, "reading *Crusade in Europe!*" It was the book he had written about the exploits of the Allied forces he commanded in North Africa, Sicily, and Europe.

The second Eisenhower-Stevenson campaign may have bored the country, but that did not necessarily make life easier for the president's secretary. As she wrote to Marie Clancy, his Philadelphia speech, for example, "was still in draft form when we got on the train—and you try to control an electric typewriter when the train is going at top speed on the Washington–Philadelphia roadbed."

"In Portland [Oregon]," Ann continued, "the truck carrying our two typewriters was run into, neither typewriter arrived at the hotel for hours, when they did neither would work, and I did the speech copy with one repairman and about ten curious civilians peering over my shoulder and the President screaming for it in the other room."

In the case of Eisenhower's speech from the White House in the final week of the campaign, Ann did not finish typing the last page until eight minutes before he went on the air. At times she was rushed into giving him pages that had not been proofread, which, she told Marie, "scares the life out of me."

Ann was angered by Stevenson's election-eve speech in Boston in which he said that "every piece of scientific evidence we have, every lesson of history and experience indicates that a Republican victory tomorrow would mean that Richard Nixon would probably be the president of this country within the next four years." "Four years ago," Ann wrote to Marie Clancy, "I had a considerable respect for Mr. Stevenson; this time none at all— and my liking for him turned to something akin to hatred for his attacks on the President's health, in such a sanctimonious manner, too."

When the votes were counted, Eisenhower did very well and Ann reasonably so, winning seven hundred dollars in a pool by coming closest to predicting the number of states her boss would carry, which was forty-two. For all her troubles with typewriters, she had found the 1956 campaign much easier than the one in 1952. "I love to travel and I love to meet people," she told Adele. "Incidentally, my newest and greatest love is Sam Goldwyn, who is a complete and utter dear. I sat next to him [at a dinner in California]. It was my one social triumph of the season."

Then things returned to normal. "The President," Ann noted, "got a new set of golf clubs from Bobby Jones, which completely delighted him. He went to Burning Tree, where he played with [Colonel] Tom Belshe and Jim Hagerty, his 'worst round of golf in his life.' " At Christmas, it was back to Augusta, but this year, on top of everything else, Ann was saddled with chores for the forthcoming second inaugural in January. As she wrote to Adele on December 28, 1956:

> For some reason—perhaps our long stay in Augusta—Christmas came upon us with a flurry and found us totally unprepared; then [a visit by] Nehru complicated our lives for days; and right in the midst of that I had to drop everything and worry about Inaugural names. Then I think I got pneumonia (*I* think it was pneumonia)—so I stayed miles away from the President but still tried to make my thick head write nice letters. You know the epitaph for my tombstone, don't you, "Write them a nice note, Ann." Don't forget.

◼9◼

On Inauguration Day in 1957 Eisenhower greeted Ann in his office with an announcement that he had not made one substantial change in the inaugural address and that no pages needed to be retyped. "This is," she happily recorded in her diary, "the most outstanding event of the past four years, from a secretary's worm's eye viewpoint." Then the president unburdened himself to her about some of his regrets at being tied down in the White House for another four years. As she wrote in her diary, she responded by trying to focus his attention on the happier side.

"He fussed for about a half hour, mainly about the responsibilities he was again undertaking and the many, many things that he and Mrs. Eisenhower wanted to do but which they would be prohibited from doing during the next four years," she noted. "Despite his frustrations, I tried to point out that he would have been a more unhappy man had he not run . . . and was this day turning the office over to Mr. Stevenson. He agreed to that premise but felt that there should have been built up another

Republican who could have won the 1956 election. I tried also the line that he is happier with responsibilities than without, but did not entirely succeed."

Ann never had any lasting doubts, however, that, fretting aside, Eisenhower liked being president. For her own part that January, she had concluded that one would have to be crazy to suppose that preparing for the inaugural festivities was fun. She had already written to Marie Clancy about having spent days "trying to fit 300 people into 200-odd seats in the President's reviewing stand, and trying to get them in proper order, protocol and such, so feelings won't be damaged." She added:

> The telephone just rang, incidentally, and Bertha Adkins wanted to know if she could bring Madame Pandit as her guest to the lunch at the Capitol and to the Reviewing Stand.* Just think of the complications that is going to cause in the diplomatic corps! So, one by one, and in the time it takes, we whittle things down. And if you hear of me being fired the day after, you will know what the cause is.

Thus the second term began.

Ann's deepest philosophical involvement in a great issue confronting President Eisenhower occurred in the summer of 1957, one of the intervals that foreshadowed the civil rights revolution of the 1960s. The particular controversies that arose in the first year of Eisenhower's second term were the debate on the civil rights bill of 1957 and the action of Governor Orval E. Faubus of Arkansas in committing the state's national guard to prevent nine black students from entering the all-white Central High School in Little Rock under a federal court order. As each of these events came to a climax, Ann talked with the president about them—without, of course, having any authority, influence, or role beyond that.

Still, the discussions were between two persons whose views and intensity of feeling on the civil rights question were

* Bertha S. Adkins was a national women's Republican leader and a future under secretary of health, education, and welfare (now health and human services). Vijaya Lakshmi Pandit was Jawaharlal Nehru's sister and a former Indian ambassador to the United States.

quite different. Eisenhower was born in Denison, Texas, and reared in the border state of Kansas. During his military career he had frequently lived on army posts in the South. After the war he became personally close to various members of the Augusta National Golf Club. Generally speaking, he had an instinctive aversion to drastic social change. In particular, he shared the concerns of white southerners over the effect on their society of legally imposed racial integration.

By contrast, in her girlhood home in Ohio Ann had been influenced by a father who had actively opposed discrimination against blacks in his township. She attended Antioch College, a most liberal school, the first president of which had been the reformer and educator Horace Mann. A few years after Ann had settled in New York, the city became a hotbed of New Deal sentiment. Her long employment with Adele Levy represented years of exposure to wealthy New York Democrats who actively supported their party and cooperated in various ways with leaders like Eleanor Roosevelt and Herbert Lehman. As secretary to the Adele R. Levy Fund, Ann acquired a certain knowledge of life in the slums. She was receptive to changes that were surely coming in American society. When she was riding on Eisenhower's campaign train in 1952, the staff had one black member, E. Frederic Morrow. Ann was surprised to learn from him that some of the secretaries aboard shunned taking his dictation. To help him out, she did it a few times when she could spare a moment from her work for the candidate. Later Morrow became an administrative officer for special projects, the only black on Eisenhower's presidential staff. He kept a diary, which was later published as a book, *Black Man in the White House*. In one entry he said that while the president could offer a job, he could not "control the minds and thoughts of the White House staff. Most of them have been correct, but cold." Nevertheless, he listed by name nine members of the staff whom he "instinctively" trusted. Ann Whitman was the first one mentioned.

She and Eisenhower had discussed the civil rights issue before the Republican National Convention in 1956, as she recorded in her diary.

[The president] said that the troubles brought about by the Supreme Court decision [in 1954, outlawing racial segregation in the public schools] were the most important problem facing the government, domestically, today. I asked the President what alternative course the Supreme Court could have adopted. He thought that perhaps they could have demanded that segregation be eliminated in graduate schools, later in colleges, later in high schools, as a means of overcoming the passionate and inbred attitudes that they [whites? southerners?] developed over generations.

A few days later the subject again rose between them.

August 19, 1956

The President said that in this [question] he was [caught] between the compulsion of duty on one side, and his firm conviction on the other, that because of the Supreme Court's ruling, the whole issue had been set back badly.

The 1957 legislation was intended, among other things, to guarantee the right to vote, meaning, especially, to southern blacks, who were virtually disenfranchised by local tests requiring them to answer preposterous questions to qualify for registration. Eisenhower was strongly in favor of this provision. Mild as the measure appears today, congressional debate raged for months. On July 10, Eisenhower conferred with the leading opponent, Senator Richard B. Russell, a Democrat from Georgia. Ann was apprehensive at the outcome, as she noted:

The President apparently indicated that he would be willing to listen to clarifying amendments to the Bill as it stands. He is not at all unsympathetic to the position people like Senator Russell take; far more ready than I am, for instance, to entertain their views. He always says, "I have lived in the South, remember." But I do think he is adamant on the fact that the right to vote must be protected.

Then Ann gave vent to her own opinion.

It seems so ridiculous to me, when it has been in the Constitution for so many years and here at last we get around to believing it might be possible for some of our citizens really to have that right.

As the showdown in Congress approached, Ann was on edge.

August 23, 1957

This is the low point in my life in the White House, but the day ended with a compromise reached on the civil rights bill which was at least a ray of hope.

Although much reduced, the bill passed. Eisenhower signed it on September 9, 1957.

If Ann's views on civil rights were much stronger than the president's, nevertheless she believed in his compassion for victims of discrimination. She understood his conflicts, springing from sympathy and concern for the white South. "You know his dilemmas as well as anyone," she was to write his friend George Allen, a Mississippian.

Governor Faubus's defiance of the law in Little Rock was the next act in the civil rights drama. In the summer of 1957 Eisenhower changed the site of his summer vacation from Denver to Newport, Rhode Island. The navy provided good working quarters for him, and Ann daily enjoyed the luxury of going to and from her job aboard the presidential yacht *Barbara Anne*.* On the day of the president's arrival he received an unwelcome telegram from Faubus. The governor pleaded for Eisenhower's understanding of his decision ordering the Arkansas national guard to prevent admission of black students to the high school in Little Rock. Eisenhower agreed to see Faubus, and the two met in Newport on September 14.

Beforehand, Ann told the president she hoped he would take a strong stand. He did not succeed in persuading Faubus to withdraw the guard. On September 24, therefore, the president ordered federal troops to Little Rock to compel the admission of the black students. He was moved to this action not out of belief in the wisdom of the Supreme Court decision or the rightness of complete racial integration at that time, but out of conviction that orders of the courts must be upheld.

* Barbara Anne Eisenhower was one of the president's three granddaughters, the other two being Susan and Mary Jean.

The coming months were hard ones for Eisenhower, especially because of the criticism he received when the Soviets beat the Americans into space with the launching of *Sputnik* on October 4, 1957. Inevitably, therefore, the period was something of a whirlwind for Ann. Before Thanksgiving, the president made a speech in Oklahoma City. Ann and Mary Caffrey received a good shaking up while typing the final draft of the talk during a turbulent flight. "It all sounds like a bad dream; and it is," Ann wrote to Madeline Earle later from Augusta. "But the President manages to survive far better than do his followers, which amazes and challenges me." She added:

"And of course the beating we take from the newspapers and radio and some of our former friends doesn't exactly lift morale. And all our friends have their own solution to the various problems, all of which I have to study through and to try to arrive at some reasonably intelligent answer. I am an authority on inflation, deflation, I'm getting outerspace conscious, and mathematical formulae long buried in memory are coming back; I am currently trying to puzzle out just where we do stand on education, scientific, I mean; I've got the Tunisian arms situation under control (in my own mind I mean all this); I cope with appointments—and remotely, Christmas presents. Sometimes I feel that I simply can't go on, but another dexamyl and I'm off to the races."

On the late flight back from Oklahoma City, Ann said, the staff knew it was the only chance they would have to get any sleep that night, and General Snyder liberally dispensed sleeping pills. She added:

> But all of us are quite certain he got hold of the wrong variety of pills; because unanimously we were wide awake during the four-hour flight back to Washington and the only girl who slept was Mary Caffrey who didn't take a pill at all.

One series of letters Ann had been taking in dictation from Eisenhower periodically since she became his secretary were addressed to Everett E. (Swede) Hazlett. Eisenhower and Hazlett had been boyhood friends in Abilene. After high school, Hazlett, who was older than Eisenhower, entered the United States Naval Academy and urged his friend to seek appointment also. In what proved to be a most important decision, Eisenhower accepted his advice, but because of a technicality over eligibility, involving his birth date, went to West Point instead. Beginning in 1941 and continuing until Captain Hazlett's death in 1958, Eisenhower wrote to him. They were strictly confidential and dwelt on Eisenhower's reactions to events and explained his motives behind his acts and his policies. Many historians now consider them a valuable resource. Without denying this, Ann tends to find them a trifle self-serving, carefully offering explanations that Eisenhower hoped history would accept. In any case, the letters were informative and reflective of the president's feelings and outlook. Thus in a letter of November 18, 1957, Eisenhower observed:

> I must tell you that physically I seem to stand up under the burden remarkably well. Yesterday I think the doctor said my blood pressure was 130 over 80 and my pulse something on the order of 66. . . .
>
> I manage to keep at least the shreds of a once fairly good disposition—a matter on which Mrs. Whitman may write you a minority report—and all in all feel that the job is being done about as well as it can be under the circumstances.

In the days following the letter, a number of things tested his disposition. He was disturbed by an interview on intercontinental ballistic missiles given to James B. Reston of *The New York Times* by General Maxwell D. Taylor, chief of staff of the army. Then an article in the *New York Herald Tribune*, long Eisenhower's favorite newspaper, angered him. The management was in a very much unsettled state at the time, and the Republican newspaper was being sharply critical of the president's policy on missiles and space. He instructed Ann to put *The New York Times* on his desk every morning from then on. But after that, she noted in her diary, November 22 was "about the worst day ever—with two very tough meetings, full of gloom and doom—Cabinet and National Security Council." The president was working on a speech scheduled to be delivered shortly in Cleveland; one night he worked late on revisions. He also had to sit through briefings on an imminent visit from the King of Morocco.

In his office on the morning of November 25, things went along about as usual. Ann thought Eisenhower looked very well. At two-forty, he returned to his office from lunch. In about ten minutes he buzzed for Ann. When she entered the Oval Office she could scarcely believe what she saw. The president was sitting at his desk, holding a letter from the wife of his friend Pete Jones, the head of Cities Service. Eisenhower was obviously confused and apparently unable to read. When, in angry frustration, he tried to talk to Ann, he was incoherent. She slipped out and directed a secretary to call Goodpaster in his nearby office and tell him to come at once. She also gave instructions that Robert Keith Gray, who was serving as appointments secretary during Stephens's absence, be notified not to admit anyone else to the Oval Office. Then Ann returned to the office and found the president still incoherent. Goodpaster, as capable a man as has ever worked in the White House, arrived. Ann scribbled a note and slipped it to him. It said, "Something terrible has happened." They called General Snyder, whose office was in the White House. Snyder told the president he wanted to take him back to the mansion. Eisenhower refused to go. "Mr. President," Goodpaster said, as he recalled his own words, "we have got to take you over to the White House and get you in bed." This time the president yielded. "Ann was in great distress," Goodpaster remembered.

Eisenhower had suffered a minor stroke. He and his family went through a wretched afternoon and evening. It took a little time for his speech to return nearly to normal. Once again he recovered remarkably well and speedily. Undoubtedly, three serious illnesses while in office took their toll on his strength, but not greatly, Ann believes. "I don't think," she said recently, "there was so much difference in his approach to problems and work after his illnesses as people make of it." After the stroke,

Ann wrote Hazlett on December 1 to reassure the navy captain about his old friend's condition. Alluding to the president's recent comment to him that she might have had a minority report to submit, she said:

"Now that I think back I could have offered a minority report. I only knew then that I was fighting a losing battle against the pace that the President seemingly compulsively set for himself. We had all ignored those hard lessons of the heart attack aftermath and everybody seemed to be dumping all the unsolvable problems squarely in his lap. . . . He was . . . wrestling with speeches at all hours of day and night, and under great pressure. . . . [A] concrete example of what I mean was the Oklahoma speech. I had no plans to go on that trip, but at noon that day the speech was still far from final. So typewriters were dumped on the plane and somehow or other we finished it. All that tends to build up in me and must for the President be magnified a thousand times, a tenseness that means loss of sleep, and a feeling always that you are not doing the job right because there simply isn't time."

As befit an old West Pointer's "good man Friday," as Goodpaster called her, she added a postscript: "Couldn't you have been generous and let Army (and the President) win yesterday?"

After resting at Gettysburg for a few days, the president returned to his office on December 2. He dictated some letters to Ann, attended part of a cabinet meeting, conferred with several officials, and hit some golf balls, she noted, "until he tried chip shots and then began to shank the balls." She added:

Despite all of our nerves for fear he was tiring himself too much, he stayed in the office until 5:45, and seemed chipper and entirely sure of himself when he left to go over to the house. He set his hat at a jaunty angle, said he thought the business of an atomic cruiser was "nuts" and walked firmly home, not nearly, seemingly, as tired as he had every right to be.*

* As of early 1988 the navy had in active service nine nuclear-powered guided missile cruisers.

He effectively silenced doubters about his health by taking off in mid-December for a nearly week-long meeting of the Atlantic Council in Paris. For her first visit to Paris Ann set out carrying a blue-and-green canvas dress bag and matching makeup case, which Adele Levy had given her as an early Christmas present. The arrival was equally felicitous for her, as the president introduced her to Charles de Gaulle, saying, as she recalled his words, "This is Mrs. Whitman without whom I couldn't live." French reporters raised their eyebrows at that statement and later pressed Merriman Smith about the meaning. He gave them the explanation they probably least wanted to hear. On her return to Washington Ann wrote to Adele to thank her for the luggage and report on Paris.

> I have only a feeling of frustration that I spent six days in that magical city and was out of the Embassy Residence one time during the daytime and that with John Eisenhower to buy his children presents. . . .
>
> But it was an experience I can never possibly forget, especially riding in the motorcade as the President entered the city. The people, mostly elderly, standing in the cold—the bitter cold—the expressions on their faces, the sheer numbers of them. It was a wonderful thing.
>
> But the rest of the time I sat in Mrs. Houghton's [Mrs. Amory Houghton, wife of the American ambassador] Petit Salon (and you know I never had a passing acquaintance with a Salon, large or small, in my life) surrounded with about 14 large wooden boxes, approximately 5 typewriters—most of which would not work on account of the [electric] current difficulty—and gifts of all descriptions. . . . And the funniest and most awful thing was that this Petit Salon trapped me. I could not get in or out during cocktails or dinner—or when the President was having his bilateral talks.
>
> Anyhow I ate watercress sandwiches for dinner, lost three pounds, and loved Paris.

◼ 10 ◼

The year 1958 was almost a career in itself for Ann, one full of ups and downs, good news and bad, hilarity and misfortune. Reading her diary for one phase is like following the zigzags on a chart of presidential laughs and frowns.

One day Eisenhower and his economics adviser, Gabriel Hauge, held a friendly, if tense, meeting with the AFL-CIO executive committee. Hauge informed Ann afterward that the labor leaders threw unfavorable statistics on the economy at Eisenhower, demanding "Why don't you act now?" Quoting Hauge, Ann wrote that Eisenhower "told them a story . . . to the effect that during the war the same thing happened—people said why don't you do something and finally he said he guessed he was too dumb to act precipitately." Apparently, Ann continued, this broke the ice with the leaders and everyone laughed.

There was no such levity in the Oval Office a few days later.

"The President received a letter from Congressman Judd [a Republican from Minnesota] which implied that Milton [Eisenhower's brother] had urged the President to reopen the Pacific airlines [route] cases, and that Milton had been influenced by Pan American. The President reacted with violent indignation and dictated a letter to Walter Judd in refutation. As of evening the letter has not been sent."

Then on another day the line on the graph soared.

"The morning was hysterical. There was to be a tree planting ceremony. . . . For a week there had been delegations on the lawn picking out the spot where the tree was to be planted.* In the morning we found a trio of workmen out to begin digging in the chosen spot. It was, quite naturally, exactly in front of the place the President uses to hit golf balls from. At this moment the President came over from the House, waved to them not to do that, to put it some '35 yards to the East.' The next thing I knew instructions had been literally followed and they were about to dig in the middle of the place where the helicopters land. We stopped that. They finally found a place."

On May 13 the line took a plunge.

"Another of the worst days of our lives. This was the day that Vice-President Nixon was attacked [by anti-American mobs] in Venezuela, that the two libraries in Lebanon were burned, that the French seemed to be in even greater trouble in Algeria than usual, for which we were being blamed, and that anti-American demonstrations were taking place in Bermuda. . . . The President said to me in mid-afternoon, 'This is bad enough, but by next week I think we'll be in even greater danger.' He also said at one point. 'I am about ready to go put my uniform on.' "

But by June the line zoomed toward a comic peak upon the occasion of the state visit of President Theodor Heuss of the Federal German Republic. Ann noted:

"This was white dinner jacket day. I can't begin, as this is written, to recount the number of phone calls, the difficulties between all the people involved—but it took another toll on an already spent female. Briefly, the story was that with the invitations to the Heuss dinner, a card was enclosed saying

* The occasion was special; each president traditionally leaves a tree planted on the White House grounds.

'white dinner jacket.' (I learned later that the season for white dinner jackets is from June first on.) Today of course was a fairly cool day and a white dinner jacket seemed a little conspicuous and out of place.

"When the President learned about it, he literally blew his top. He was going to wear his black coat, despite everything. Then we discovered that poor President Heuss was having a white coat made—rushed by the tailor—and to be safe had also bought a black one. So the President had to wear a white one, which did not please him. This matter was discussed with the President, Mrs. Eisenhower, the Secretary of State, Tom Stephens, etc., and thousands of State employees. People just would not believe the furor . . .

"The guests included a lot of dowager ladies, including Mrs. Gifford Pinchot [widow of a former governor of Pennsylvania] who wore a deep purple dress, a green scarf and carried an orange ostrich fan that (according to the newspapers) perfectly matched the color of her hair. This made my day."

The year had begun for Ann on a low note. On January 6 Eisenhower ended a ten-day stay in Gettysburg to return to Washington in time for the opening of the new session of Congress. While Ann was packing at the old Gettysburg Hotel, the motorcade suddenly left from the farm. She jumped into her car and set off in a roar to overtake it. Rolling into Maryland at eighty miles an hour, she was arrested, given a stiff lecture on the road, but later a mere official warning. The story of the arrest of the president's secretary went out, to Ann's lasting resentment, on the Associated Press wire. "I was in bad odor around the Oval Office for several days," she recalled. That attitude seemed a little bit overdone. Once on a trip to Gettysburg the speedometer in the limousine in which the wire service reporters were riding registered one hundred miles an hour, as the driver strove to keep up with Eisenhower's car.

A few weeks later, in March, Ann received some publicity of a different sort in a *New York Herald Tribune* article on the husbands of "famous" wives. The series included articles on the spouses of Marian Anderson and Risë Stevens, opera singers;

Irene Dunne, an actress; Ivy Baker Priest, the treasurer of the United States, and Anne Fogarty, a fashion designer. The second in the series was on Edmund Whitman. He responded with a light touch to an interview by Keith R. Johnson. "I've given the best years of my wife to the Republican party," he quipped. And to those who, he said, told him, "Whenever I want to see the president, I have to talk to your wife," he replied, "Well, every time I want to talk to my wife I have to see the president." He expressed pleasure at having met "most of the people in the inner circle of the White House." He recalled that he had been with Ann a number of times in Augusta, Gettysburg, and Denver. "But," he added, "she's quiet, and never talks about what she does. She wouldn't be as good at the job if she did." In retrospect, however, some of his words have a slightly plaintive ring.

"In a sense," he said, "I haven't really seen my wife since she went to Denver 'for two weeks' in 1952 . . . almost six years ago. It's a lonely life for me. I'm on my own a lot. It's not a satisfactory relationship at all. But my wife is in duty bound to serve the President as long as he needs her, and I lead a full life—my job is interesting and time-consuming as well, and I have no time to sit around."

The good fortune for Ann was that one day during the year Eisenhower idly picked up the *Federal Register* and chanced upon a list of salaries paid to leading government secretaries. What he saw caused him to grab the telephone, call Maurice H. Stans, the new budget director, and remonstrate that some other officials' secretaries were paid more than his. Ann's salary, which had been creeping up for five years from the original $7,000, was soon given a substantial boost, and by the time the administration left office in January 1961 she was earning around $15,000 a year. No one doubted that she earned it.

In July 1958 Ann accompanied Eisenhower on the second of his two visits to Ottawa. On the first one, in 1953, she had found the Canadian capital and its people drab. This time, as she said in her diary, the city "was really lovely, the government buildings impressive." In a ceremony at the National War

Memorial, during which Eisenhower delivered what Ann called an "awfully good" speech, he "assumed that military bearing that I so love."

That was the summer of one of the most jolting episodes in the eight years of the Eisenhower administration. A subcommittee of the House Committee on Interstate and Foreign Commerce created a sensation by accusing Sherman Adams, the assistant to the president—Eisenhower's chief of staff—of conflict of interest. The subcommittee charged that Adams had allowed Bernard Goldfine, a New England textile manufacturer, to pay some hotel bills for him in Boston. Furthermore, Adams had made a call to the Securities and Exchange Commission on behalf of Goldfine, who was in difficulty over taxes and government regulations. On the face of it, this was an unacceptable exercise of influence by a government official on behalf of a friend or benefactor. Adams was unable to quell the criticism by testifying that the only thing he had done for Goldfine was to make one telephone call to the SEC, asking that its hearings in the case be expedited. And if there was a mitigating factor in Adams's conduct, which he himself later called imprudent, it was that in his years in the New Hampshire legislature, in Congress, and as governor, he, like other New England governors and legislators, had been accustomed to helping Goldfine and other industrialists prosper in order to provide badly needed jobs in New England. If Goldfine had paid Adams's hotel bill, Adams had in the past, he said, entertained Goldfine.

Ann liked and admired Adams. As a senior member of the White House she attended his daily staff meetings when she was not tied up with the president. Contrary to some accounts, Adams was not a man disliked in the White House by practically everyone but Eisenhower. "I never knew anyone in the White House who didn't like Governor Adams," Ann said afterward. Doubtless there were some, but there were many others who admired him deeply. A taught, stern, industrious New Englander, he was so intolerant of wasted time that he habitually hung up on telephone conversations the instant he either had the information he wanted or had delivered his own message. "He even hung up once on me," Eisenhower laughingly told Roemer McPhee. Adams was a formidable figure in the White House. He had the authority, or often assumed it, to call around the government and say "The president wants ____." This is a great deal of authority indeed. Adams did not do only that which the president asked him to, but also, acting independently, that which he judged the president would want or, in the end, approve. Ann once wrote that in a system designed to bring before the president options collectively selected by the staff for his consideration before final action was taken, Adams "frequently made unilateral decisions." Under pressure he could be a rock. Unlike many who have sat in high places in Washington over the years, he was known to carry out commitments he had made, though the ground might shake under him.

In her 1955 letter to the president of the *Nashville Banner* concerning the White House staff, Ann said that Adams was often used as a scapegoat. In other words, he was the lightning rod for criticism intended for Eisenhower by politicians and others who had no stomach for affronting a popular president. Few of Adams's critics, Ann wrote, "ever took into consideration the size of the job he was holding down, the lack of precedent in it, the massive pressures sustained by him through long days and nights—and at the same time his wife was very ill in the hospital."*

"If those who criticized him could have known all the facts" she concluded, "I think every one of them who possessed honesty and integrity would say of him, regardless of personal prejudice: 'This sort of man doesn't happen often enough for the good of the country.' "

Eisenhower did not think Adams had done anything crooked. The president, in fact, was shocked and depressed by his belief

---

* Concerning precedent, Ann was both right and wrong. Dr. John R. Steelman had been the assistant to President Harry S Truman—an unprecedented title. But Steelman's authority was not comparable to that of Adams's when he held the same title.

that Adams's accusers knew Adams was an honest man. At a press conference Eisenhower defended his assistant's integrity and said "I need him." Nevertheless, the hearings continued to turn up charges, the most newsworthy being that Adams had accepted a gift of a vicuña coat from Goldfine. This was a delicious discovery for the Democrats. In the 1952 campaign the Eisenhower forces had pilloried them over a Democratic political operator giving an $8,540 royal pastel mink coat to an obscure White House stenographer. The Republicans turned the coat into a supreme symbol of corruption in the Truman administration. That was the purpose of Nixon's statement in his famous "Checkers" speech in which he defended himself against allegations of having a trust fund, saying that his wife did not "have a mink coat. But she does have a respectable Republican cloth coat." Adams's predicament was worsened by the fact that his Republican enemies used his embarrassment to demand his dismissal. Their pressure on Eisenhower to that end was greatly strengthened by the fact that congressional elections were scheduled for that November. The Adams case, they insisted, might cause the Republican party to lose seats in Congress.

Eisenhower's friend from the Augusta National Golf Club, New York stockbroker Cliff Roberts, regarded himself as a considerable authority on Republican politics. Before leaving on a trip to Europe in June, Roberts wrote a letter to Adams urging him to resign in the interest of the party. Adams's secretary, Mary Burns, who opened the letter, was so shocked she did not show it to him. Instead, she sent it to Ann with a note asking whether it might be appropriate for Ann or Stephens to return the letter to Roberts, intimating that he might wish to withdraw it altogether.

"Foolishly," Ann wrote in her diary on July 14, 1958, "I kept the letter, since Mr. Roberts was away. I did tell the President about the letter. When we were in Ottawa . . . Andy Tully [a reporter for the Scripps-Howard newspapers] called me, saying there was a story the President had, in retaliation for this letter, which had somehow leaked, resigned from the Augusta National. That Augusta story I denied."

When Roberts returned from Europe, Ann had lunch with him "and had to tell him the story." Adams had not yet seen his letter. Roberts, Ann noted, "was angry, I thought, but did not violently upbraid me." Eisenhower reprimanded her mildly, and she returned the letter to Mary Burns. Then Roberts wrote a second letter, this one to the president, arguing that the Republican party would be hurt badly if Adams remained. As Ann watched the drama unfold, it was this letter, she judged, that led to Adams's downfall. After reading it, Eisenhower told her the Adams affair was a cause of "hopelessness" in its accumulating effect on the party. His conclusion, she recalled, was reinforced by a conversation in the same vein in Newport that September with Winthrop W. Aldrich, a former chairman of the board of the Chase National Bank and former United States ambassador to the Court of St. James's. Eisenhower told Ann that Adams "has got to go or we [the Republican party] are done." The president stood aside and allowed the party hierarchy to force Adams to resign. Nevertheless, in the congressional elections in November the Republicans suffered the worst defeat of its kind since the start of the Depression.

With Newport behind her, Ann was soon back at her grind, typing a speech text, this one dealing with more troubles in the Formosa Strait.

"At any rate," she wrote to Marie Clancy on September 12, 1958, "we arrived in Washington yesterday afternoon, at four o'clock—when the Secretary [Dulles] got there—with three distinct and different drafts, all with changes on them—and the problem to get them coordinated. I almost lost my mind and got exceedingly confused. Finally we got a workable draft done, say 6:15, then came the reading copy (which is the bane of my life). . . .

"Much fun. That took a couple of hours and just as I sent it bouncing over, the Pres was on the phone inquiring rather testily WHERE in hell was his speech. Then he comes over 45 minutes before the broadcast and usually you sweat out retyping half a dozen pages. (Some day I am going to find myself crawling hands on knees out of range of the camera to hand him the final half dozen pages as he bravely talks to the nation.)"

She added a description of dinner at Trader Vic's on a recent weekend in New York:

> I never have felt so much like a hick and never been so astounded at the shortness of dresses and the absolute different look (I guess the Bridgitte Bardot look) of some of the females on the street. I am definitely feeling my age; not around here, thank goodness, because everybody wears their old clothes.

Then a trip in early November to Seattle for another foreign policy speech by the president earned a disdainful note in Ann's diary.

"The entire trip was marred by a series of instances such as: The Secretary of State selling the President on not going to Seattle, as he had wanted, on Sunday evening (frankly because the Secretary wanted the President's suite at the Olympic Hotel); the State Department insisting they would not release the speech until the Secretary had approved the final changes and Jim Hagerty's equal insistence that once the President had approved, that was it; the State Department's having a formal briefing on the speech here in Washington Friday without telling Jim about it; no place in the hotel for the President to go except the Manager's Office; no seats for the White House staff while Phyliss Bernau [one of Dulles's secretaries] sat gaily in the second row. All little things, but all adding up to the thought which I fully share—that the State Department regards the President as its chattel."

Toward the end of 1958, Ann had a couple of contrasting experiences with social affairs. In mid-November, she and Whit were invited to a dinner party at the home of Under Secretary of State Bedell Smith. Whit was particularly pleased with the invitation and bought Ann a mink stole for the occasion. But then, as she wrote to Marie Clancy, the party was called off "because I got all that notoriety in the Drew Pearson column." The column was occasioned by a question asked of the president at a recent press conference. The question concerned a familiar complaint that the United Fruit Company used its economic power to influence and often dominate weak Central American governments, creating animosity toward the United States in that region. The query rather irked Eisenhower, but not so much as the column. Pearson wrote:

> What most newsmen who heard [Eisenhower's] irritation didn't know is that Ike's confidential secretary is married to a top United Fruit executive. Ann Whitman, who shares the President's secrets and exercises a quiet influence on him, is the wife of United Fruit's public relations boss, Ed Whitman.

"The president was furious about that column," Ann recalled. "I never discussed the United Fruit Company with him."

Eisenhower of course knew where her husband worked.

Before Christmas, on the other hand, Ann had a good time at the Nixons'. "The party was fun (even though the Vice-President forced on me too many of his 6-to-1 martinis)," she related in the aforementioned letter to Mrs. Clancy. "Then we went off to a restaurant and the first thing I know he and Mrs. Nixon joined us. I proceeded to carry on at a great rate (I can't remember what it was all about this morning) and actually I woke up feeling fine, for some strange reason. He is fun to be with and the amazing part of it is that he manages to go around town without too many people staring at him or bothering him. I only wish the Pres . . . had his freedom."

■ 11 ■

Soon the geographic limits of Ann's job were stretched because, in the summer of 1959, a new dimension was added to the presidency: Eisenhower became the first president to have a jet plane. His propeller-driven *Columbine II*, itself a successor to Franklin Roosevelt's *Sacred Cow* and Harry S Truman's *Independence*, was replaced by the newly designated *Air Force One*, a four-engine Boeing 707 jet transport.

Before the advent of the jet plane, practical reasons strictly limited how far presidents could travel abroad and how long they could stay away. With the jet, however, no place was more than hours from Washington. Hence a president could return from abroad quickly in case of emergency. This facility suddenly made it possible for presidents, beginning with Eisenhower, to project themselves and their influence, which they have done with relish, especially since such journeys are featured on television news at home. In Eisenhower's case, for instance, his last eighteen months in office were conspicuous for prolonged and historic presidential visits to India, East Asia, and South America, and for longer stays in Europe.

What this meant for Ann was the exhilaration of flying over the Khyber Pass or of visiting the Parthenon in Athens. It also meant the exhaustion of taking dictation and turning out letters while, on a couple of occasions, landing on three different continents on the same day. And it meant some exotic confusions that no presidential secretary before her could have imagined. The forthcoming trips were to add great variety to a job that already seemed constantly to transport her between the comic and the grave, with stops in between at boredom, tension, political conflict, eccentric personalities, and the puzzle of increasing presidential mood changes.

In the midst of one difficult time in 1959, President Seán T. O'Kelly (O'Ceallaigh) of Ireland arrived as a guest of the Eisenhowers on St. Patrick's Day. "When Mrs. Eisenhower called and invited me to come to the dinner," Ann wrote, "I had no dress but scurried over to Garfinkel where the selection was anything but good. I finally got a red one that I liked very much, but it is an expensive $125 worth of an evening." There was no time for alterations. Later, when she was getting ready for the arrival of her escort for the evening, Leonard Hall, she could not quite fit herself into the dress. The Republican national chairman, however, managed to "zip" her into it.

Shamrocks, white ties, and a profusion of green evening gowns filled the White House. "The whole affair was to me a sort of starry-eyed wonder," Ann observed in her diary, "but the President of Ireland held up the proceedings greatly by (1) insisting on kissing every pretty lady, (2) shaking hands with all the ushers and photographers he could see, and (3) talking interminably during the dinner. As a result Fred Waring [the band leader] started late, and, of course, he could not stop at all. The musical program was finished a little after 12:00. I was dead, and President Eisenhower admitted he was too."

What made the spring of 1959 a particularly hard time for Eisenhower was the grave condition of John Foster Dulles's health. Because Ann spent so much time in the Oval Office, she was exposed to the president's feelings and noted his comments. She also was touched by emotion over Dulles's rapid decline because she had seen a great deal of him during the previous six years. Even those around the president, including Ann, who resented what they thought was Dulles's restraining influence on Eisenhower's own instincts for accommodation with the Soviets liked the secretary of state personally.

"He had, when with the President," she wrote to George Allen, "a truly warm personality and there was an easy friendship between the two of them. While Dulles did look dour and forbidding at times, there was unexpected fun and lack of reserve behind that exterior."

One day Ann and Goodpaster were talking with Eisenhower when mention was made of Dulles, and Eisenhower spoke of the differences between himself and the secretary with respect to dealing with the Soviets. Ann quoted Eisenhower:

His is a lawyer's mind. He consistently adheres to a very logical explanation of these difficulties in which we find ourselves with the Soviets and in doing so—with his lawyer's mind—he shows the steps and actions that are bad on their part; and we seek to show that we are doing the decent and just thing. Of course we have got to have a concern and respect for fact and reiteration of official position, but we are likewise trying to "seek friends and influence people."

Therefore (I sometimes question) the practice of becoming a sort of international prosecuting attorney in which I lay out all of the things that I intend to prove before the grand jury and make an opening statement of intention in order to make certain that people will understand.

Whatever history's ultimate judgment of Dulles may be, he was a commanding figure in Washington and in the other capitals of the world in the 1950s. Toward the end of 1956 he had to undergo surgery for abdominal cancer. After several weeks of convalescence he returned to his duties, vigorously. By early 1959, however, he was again tormented by pain and was growing weak. On February 14 the president visited him in Walter Reed Hospital.

"Obviously," Ann noted in her diary, "he is hard hit by the business about Dulles. He said that if he accepted his resignation, however, he doubted if Dulles would live for more than a few weeks. . . .

"Mostly the President does not dwell on death, and, indeed, I have seen him rarely shaken by the death, or thought of death, of any of his closest friends. But this morning he did talk a little bit about it, mentioned General Persons's father-in-law who one night this week had a couple of drinks, had a good dinner and died in his sleep—that is so much the better way to die. It seems so wrong somehow that a man who has given of himself as Secretary Dulles did must die in such a painful fashion, held up every moment to the world's prying eyes. Somehow it makes you wonder whether it is all worth it."

During a series of telephone calls on February 16 between the president and the secretary, Dulles got Ann on the line and, as she noted, "thanked me formally for my part in the 'association'—I dissolved in tears, of course."

Four days later Eisenhower again saw Dulles and, Ann noted, returned in a "queer mood" —"seemed to want only to be left alone, said he was 'talked out,' that he wanted to 'mope' around alone. I had to ask him a couple of questions during the afternoon and he seemed unhappy at being disturbed."

Soon Dulles decided that he must resign, and at his suggestion Eisenhower appointed as his successor Under Secretary of State Christian A. Herter of Massachusetts, who was sworn in on April 22, 1959. "Mrs. Dulles, looking very composed, attended the ceremony," Ann recorded. "I understand she drove down to the White House in the car of the Secretary of State (with the State Department seal on the side), then turned the car over to Mr. Herter and went home with Douglas Dillon." Former ambassador to France, Dillon became the new under secretary of state. Dulles died on May 24.

Thus within a span of several months two men who in different ways had been commanding figures in the Eisenhower administration, Dulles and Adams, disappeared from the scene. On the surface at least the new order brought change. It loosened procedures in the White House. Ann was among those whose role would be affected.

Ann once wrote to Adele Levy that "pack, unpack, and repack is the rule of my life." This was true enough as preparations began for Eisenhower's departure on August 26, 1959, on the first of his jet tours, this one to Western Europe. Beforehand, Ann was mired in work in Gettysburg. In a cloudy mood she wrote to Marie Clancy:

"This Bonn-London-Paris trip is going to be upon us before we know it. I need a permanent and no time to get one. I need a lot of clothes and am really stuck here. But neither will matter since I shall be confined to the Embassies in the latter two cities and probably not see the sights at all, or even the light of day. Glamorous job some people call it. To that I say bosh and bosh and more bosh. I think I probably told you I lived on watercress sandwiches when we were in Paris before, standing on one foot all the while, incidentally. This new wrinkle of living at the Embassies which the President threw at me the other day presents a few more problems since I am neither fish nor fowl, if you know what I mean. But I am thrilled to be going to England."

By the time of departure she was back in good spirits. Her notes both reflected her fascination with every aspect of her first flight on a jet and evoked memories of the wonder and comforts, now largely forgotten, of the coming of jet-age travel. She found the Boeing 707 much more spacious and comfortable than the Lockheed Constellation. "There are four washrooms," she noted, "and I must say I was impressed by flush toilets!"

"Personally," she recalled, "the most exciting part of the trip was going up to the controls and sitting right behind Bill Draper and the second pilot. . . . I put the earphones on and heard all the communication between planes in the area (we were going over England). Very exciting when London would call 'Air Force One' and Air Force One (Tommy sitting beside me) would reply."

She was surprised at the number of parks she could see in the sprawl of London and was soon excited by the sight of the white cliffs of Dover. "Most notable thing," she said, "was the difference in types of architecture in Germany; also something I had not seen before (in flying over Belgium) was the way the land was laid out in 'strips.'

"At Bonn on the dot, of course, and the President was greeted by the Chancellor [Konrad Adenauer], looking exceedingly spry and handsome and vigorous for his 83 years."

The twenty-seven-mile drive from the Cologne-Bonn Airport to the city of Bonn was exhilarating. To those who thought about it, this was surely due in part to the fact that, as Ann wrote afterward, Eisenhower was "cheered by young, pink-cheeked, blue-eyed Germans against [whose country] he had been fighting fifteen or sixteen years [before]." Shouts of *"wunderbar"* and "We like Ike" welled up around the motorcade. The steeples of Cologne Cathedral were visible through the haze of a plain. "We went through little town after little town, all jammed," Ann recorded in her diary. "In Siegburg, for instance, with a population of some 25,000, the estimate of people was over 50,000. Apparently people had come from all parts of Germany to see—and genuinely welcome—the President. I rode in a car with Mrs. [David K. E.] Bruce, wife of the ambassador [to the Federal Republic of Germany], Mr. Timberlake, who is the Minister of the Embassy, and Tom Stephens. We all waved constantly (and tiring even for us)."

The next day Ann joined the president at the Schaumburg Palace, where he spent hours conferring with Adenauer. "At one point," she noted, "I was in the room assigned to me as an office—and as usual boxes and packages and things were all over the floor. To my complete surprise and that of everyone else, the President and Chancellor appeared from a door that we thought was tightly locked and both had to run an obstacle course to get to the suite provided for the President for resting. . . . To avoid the return long trip through crowds to the airport, the President requested helicopters, and they were supplied by the Army in Frankfurt. When I came to get [aboard], I found that it was utterly impossible. The first step was a good three feet off the ground and with a short tight skirt there was just no way to get on. John Eisenhower picked me up by the waist and bodily lifted me in—this in front of hundreds of people."

That afternoon, August 27, 1959, Eisenhower flew to London to be cheered by what were said to be the largest crowds in the streets since the coronation of Queen Elizabeth II six years earlier. Patrons flowed from pubs to watch the president and Macmillan pass in a gray-and-silver Rolls-Royce; pints were hoisted to them in front of the Bunch of Grapes on Duke Street. Indeed entire neighborhoods seemed to turn out. In the excitement around the motorcade a red-headed woman was thrown from a white horse in Hyde Park.

"We passed an overpass under construction," Ann recalled in her diary, "and Philip de Zueleta [a secretary to the prime minister] said seriously that it was too bad it had not been finished in time. Andy Goodpaster remembers distinctly that the same overpass has been under construction since 1955 at least, and that when he was last in London, about a year ago, it looked precisely as it now looks.

"But despite that everybody in London looks much the same as we do—well dressed, lipstick, high heels, short skirts. There are relatively few traces of bombing—one or two buildings I did see that had not been torn down or rebuilt."

The following day the president went to Balmoral Castle to spend the night with the royal family. As he rolled along a road in the Scottish highlands from the airport to the castle, a never more appropriate sight was seen than that of some men in tweeds presenting arms to him with golf clubs. As a personal gift the president gave Queen Elizabeth a clock radio. When plugged in, it did not work. Behind-the-scenes frenzy on both sides of the Atlantic Ocean produced a replacement within thirty-six hours. Fortunately for Ann, who had stayed in London with most of the rest of the staff, the burden of accomplishing this feat fell on the navy's shoulders, not hers. She was free to see the city for the first time, as a typical tourist, retreating only before the Tower of London because the cobblestones were too much for her three-inch heels. Ann was drawn to England because her mother's parents came from there. The next day was the loveliest of the trip, as she, Goodpaster, and Secretary of State Herter drove together through the countryside to Chequers, country residence of prime ministers. They made the trip to join Eisenhower and Macmillan for the weekend. Ann wrote to Whit, who was recovering from diverticular surgery:

> Principally my reaction is one of wonder and awe because of the age and history of the place, and one of being downright cold most of the time. It is proving to be a very relaxed weekend, I think for the President, and the Prime Minister is even unbending. Last night when I went into the movie room, he got up and so did all the party, [which] unnerved me completely.

On her return to Washington on September 9, Ann raved about the trip in a letter to Mrs. Levy. "I shan't bore you with any part of it," she said, "but just imagine Ann Cook of Perry, Ohio, sleeping in the room at Chequers in which Lady Mary Gray was imprisoned for two years back in 1565. (No rattling of chains was heard.)"*

After a theatrical welcome in Paris on September 2, in which de Gaulle hailed him as the liberator of France and huge crowds in the boulevards responded appropriately, Eisenhower ended his European stay in the town of Turnberry Point, Scotland. There, perched on a sheer cliff rising from the Firth of Clyde, stood Culzean (pronounced Cul-lane) Castle, in which Eisenhower had a sixteen-room apartment on the third floor for life, the gift of the Scottish people to the supreme Allied commander. Not far from the castle, which had been built in 1777, stretched a golf course along the Atlantic Ocean. The different holes had such names as "Blaw Wearie," "Fin Me Oot," "Tappie Tourie," "Roon the Ben," "Dinna Fouter," "Tickley

---

* Lady Mary was the sister of the more unfortunate Lady Jane Gray, who, in civil strife, was beheaded after nine days as Queen of England.

Tap," "Ca Canny," and "Lang Whang." And just as at Burning Tree, Augusta, Palm Springs, and Pebble Beach, members of Eisenhower's gang—"Ike's millionaires," according to a contemporary press room ditty—were in Scotland to join him when it came time for the president to tee off. Jock Whitney, then ambassador to the Court of St. James's, came from London and Bill Robinson and Pete Jones from New York.

One night Eisenhower gave a dinner in the castle for British and American guests, including Ann. As she settled down at the table, she was surprised when the president almost barked at General Snyder, "Howard, put that out!" Equally surprised, no doubt, the president's physician extinguished his cigarette. Eisenhower proceeded to give the American guests a lecture on the discourtesy of smoking before the offering of a toast to the queen. "I practically held my head in shame," recalled Ann, who was not smoking herself but was crushed that her colleagues had to be reprimanded at such a time. All things considered, Eisenhower's lecture was a bit overblown. In 1942 he had scarcely arrived in London as the American commander in the European Theater when the United States Ambassador, James Winant, gave a dinner party for him. The next morning the ambassador called Eisenhower for an appointment. When Winant arrived, he politely explained that the American commander had violated custom at the dinner by smoking a cigarette before the toast to the king.

After a flight from Prestwick, Scotland, Eisenhower and his staff returned to the White House about 2 P.M. on September 7. He worked in his office for a couple of hours. The sequel Ann confided to her diary: "Mind you, we had been up some 18 hours. But when the President left at around 4:00 o'clock—this was a Labor Day holiday—he said to me, generously, 'Take the rest of the afternoon off!' "

Planning was soon well along for Eisenhower's trip to India and ten other countries in Asia, Africa, and Europe, a 22,730-mile journey such as had never before been seen in the history of the presidency. Ann volunteered to handle the task of lining up the gifts and photographs of himself that Eisenhower would distribute on his seventeen-day odyssey. "I should have thought twice," she rued in her diary.

"There never has been pressure like this or details like these," she wrote to Adele Levy. "For instance—the gifts, mostly of Steuben glass or silver or desk set variety, all have to be engraved and wrapped. The photographs *have* to be in three different categories—for Head of State (largest and silver frame with seal); for Head of Government, approximately same size but different pose, and leather frame with seal; for Foreign Ministers (to me the number 3 guy), a cheaper frame and a still different photograph. All have to be inscribed and wrapped and sorted. Then there is a small matter of a Polaroid camera and letter to go with it. Then there are gifts for hostesses, all engraved. And if the gift for the Queen of Greece doesn't end up in Afghanistan I shall be mightily fooled."

Ann feared that the burden of handling gifts would restrict sightseeing for her, and she was not altogether wrong. For just as she, along with the State Department, was responsible for arranging the gifts that Eisenhower would present, so she was also responsible for thanking the kings, queens, princes, princesses, and foreign ministers for those they would give him. "Gift letters," she wrote later. "DDE policy of course. To be delivered by hand by embassy personnel, if abroad." This meant that in each capital Ann would have to write the letters and get them in the embassy's hands before rushing to the plane for the next fifteen-hundred-mile flight. Of course, she could finish letters only to the most important personages at most stops. The record shows that on August 15, 1960, eight months later, she was still exchanging letters about gifts with American embassies, and the task was not yet finished. For weeks after the trip ended, cargo planes were hauling back gifts. These included a conglomeration of such household necessities as an elephant from India, an Arab stallion and two gazelles from Tunis, a four-foot tree of silver filigree from Pakistan, and bejeweled shotguns from Spain.

The first leg of the trip was from Washington to Rome for a

short stay. Characteristically, Ann's feeling of harassment was instantly replaced by one of excitement and adventure the moment the wheels of the plane touched down on December 4 in heavy rain. Enthralled by the new sights about her, she later wrote in her diary:

"The ride in was fabulous, on the old Appian Way. The road was lined with what I guess were the tombs of Caesar's soldiers. You could see the remnants of the viaduct—we came past the Colosseum, I was told where the Forum was. Later I saw the part of the old Roman wall. . . . what beats me is how they have adjusted the modern age to the antiquities about them—traffic weaving beneath the old Roman wall for instance."

Then disappointment rushed in when the president reached the four-hundred-year-old Quirinal Palace, which stands on one of the seven hills of Rome and is the official residence of the president of Italy. President Eisenhower was a guest there. The expectation was that Ann also would be put up in the palace, but to her annoyance she found herself domiciled in the Grand Hotel with the rest of the White House staff and the press. She was given to understand, with what effect on a former member of the Lucy Stone League may be imagined, that the Italians would not assign a room in the Quirinal Palace to a woman secretary. It may have been some consolation, but not much, that Eisenhower escorted her up and showed her his resplendent bedroom, with its ceiling painted with religious imagery.

After they had unpacked, Ann, Mary Caffrey, and Kevin McCann went out for a quiet dinner. It turned out to be Ann's first dinner that night. Around midnight she was awakened by a call from Merriman Smith, who with Stewart Hensley, a colleague from United Press International, insisted on taking her to dinner with them. "The place they took me," according to her diary, "was filled with people who had been at the reception . . . at the Palace . . . the women are very glamorous, much eye make up etc. The hairdos are incredible."

The next day things were bleak again:

"My 'office' at the Quirinale will always remain a bad nightmare. Yesterday it was approximately ten feet by three feet;

today it has been enlarged (actually it is the cloak room of the Palace). But there is a steady procession of men carrying large boxes of dishes in and out—and the door must remain open; I have had—this is 4:30 in the afternoon—one apple, one peppermint patty and some cheese plus coffee all day long. It is barren and the door makes it cold. The lighting is horrible. I had no bathroom until finally I demanded one. I am here all day alone and feel forsaken."

The next day, when the president was scheduled to take off for Turkey, could not have been plotted by Rube Goldberg. Its principal ingredients were two papal audiences and an Italian chauffeur.

The first audience Pope John XXIII held was for the press and most of the White House staff and Secret Service. The second and later one was for the president and a few other passengers on *Air Force One*, which would have included Ann. This was held directly before Eisenhower's scheduled departure for the airport. Not only was Ann not particularly interested in attending, but she also thought she had better allow herself plenty of time to get to the airport with the boxes of the president's classified papers, which were entrusted to her care. As she well knew, any delay in takeoff was beyond the pale.

Hurriedly, therefore, she checked out of the Grand Hotel with her luggage and the boxes of classified documents and climbed into a limousine sent by the American embassy. The limousine had barely pulled away when the press bus arrived for those attending the first audience in the Sistine Chapel. In the front seat was Mary Caffrey with a paper bag full of medals and rosaries. A number of the reporters, photographers, and Secret Service agents wanted to take religious objects for the pope to bless but had had no time to shop. Mary had volunteered to do the shopping for them. Just as the bus was about to leave, someone from the White House transportation crew rushed out of the hotel, waving something blue in the air. He jumped into the bus and told Mary, "Mrs. Whitman left these in her room." He handed Mary a pair of pajamas. Not knowing what else to do with them, as all the baggage had gone ahead, she stuffed them in the bag with the rosaries and medals. At the proper moment during the audience, she held up the bag, and Pope John pronounced a blessing on its contents.

Meanwhile Ann discovered that the driver of the embassy limousine was an Italian. When they reached the airport, he did not know where *Air Force One* was waiting, and neither did Ann. At first they drove around, wasting valuable time. The president would be rushed to the airport as soon as the second audience was over. While some may suppose it preposterous not to be able to locate a Boeing 707 on the ground, on the contrary, such a search can be utterly frustrating. International airports are sprawling, busy places. Dozens of buildings cut off views. Fences hinder. Buses interfere. Among scores of aircraft on the ground, it can be difficult to pick out a particular plane, especially when, as in the case of *Air Force One*, it was parked more or less out of sight from the roadways in a secure area away from other traffic. Thus, while the president would soon take off for Ankara, all his secret records and his secretary were riding around in circles, unable to find the plane.

It was apparent to Ann that she would have to do one of two things without further delay. Either she would have to get out of the car and get directions, thereby violating regulations by leaving classified papers with an unauthorized person, in this case a foreign national unknown to her. Or else she would have to send the driver for directions, although he might not return in time for the takeoff. And she knew what that might mean. In a letter to Adele Levy on September 23, 1953, she had related an incident in Chicago when the car in which she was riding became separated from the motorcade on the way to the airport and caught up with the president only at the last moment. "You know," she wrote, "the rule is when the President arrives at the airplane everybody else must be on board, he goes up the steps, and whsst—off the plane goes." To have missed this plane would have been a calamity for Ann. She resolved her dilemma. "I felt guilty leaving the papers untended with that driver," she recalled, "but I had to get out and inquire." She and the records were both on board when President Eisenhower took off.

The president received a demonstrative welcome in Ankara, Turkey, where men in bright native dress danced in the streets. Buildings were festooned with signs, one of which read WELCOME AIK. As the tour progressed beyond Western Europe, millions of people along the way did not know the name of the president of the United States, but they knew, or seemed to have a good idea, who "Ike" was. His nickname was universal. *"Zindabad* [long live] *Ike!"* filled the air in the next stop, Karachi. It was chanted by thousands of Pakistanis, including men in fezzes or "jinnah caps" and women in saris of lavender or pink or lemon. Karachi was an absorbing scene. As the motorcade passed through areas of squalor, eyes could be seen peering at the president, wonderingly, through slits in mud huts. Yet not far away the American visitors were transported into the world of Rudyard Kipling, watching thundering mounted lancers in an exhibition of tent-pegging or the slow cadence of a cricket match on a pretty green. It was a day on which Russell Baker, *The New York Times* reporter on the trip, banished any doubt about his claim to have been a great high hurdler in high school. When a man sidled up to him with a large burlap bag, peddling his wares, which, upon inspection, turned out to be a mass of writhing snakes, Baker crossed a main thoroughfare in half a dozen bounds.

Back aboard *Air Force One*, flying to Kabul, capital of Afghanistan, Ann sat with the pilots for a view of the Khyber Pass. Images were formed in her memory that day that caused her to be surprised twenty years later when President Jimmy Carter and others were shocked by the Soviets' invasion of Afghanistan. "They were always there," she said later. Soviet-built MiG fighters with Afghan pilots escorted Eisenhower's airplane on the approach to the Soviet-constructed Bagram Airport. From there it was an hour's drive to Kabul through an ancient-looking land dominated by the snow-covered Hindu Kush Mountains. At crossroads, schoolchildren and clusters of herdsmen, shepherds, and farmers waved at Eisenhower. Now and then he passed a nomadic man and woman and donkey, their appearance resembling scenes already flooding the mails at home on Christmas cards depicting Mary and Joseph arriving in Bethlehem.

Eisenhower lunched with King Mohammed Zahir Shah at the Chilistoon Palace on a mountain outside the capital. On the road leading to it the façades of the buildings and houses had been whitewashed, conveying the impression of a certain prosperity. Ann was quick to notice that the drab sidewalls and backs remained unwashed. She and Mary Caffrey were served lunch in a different part of the palace from where the president and the king were. When it came time for the president to leave, someone was tardy about informing the two women. The spectators outside were to behold the spectacle of two unveiled secretaries, half running, half staggering in high heels down a steep cobblestone street to keep from being left behind at the end of the world.

In New Delhi on that same evening of December 10, 1959, the president was mobbed by adoring crowds in a motorcade en route from Palam Airport to the Rashtrapati Bhavan, literally the abode of the chief of the nation. The 345-room edifice, covering nearly five acres, had been built in the 1920s for the viceroys of British India, the last of them having been Eisenhower's friend, Lord Mountbatten. It had taken more than two hours for the police, the Secret Service, and the drivers of the vehicles to force their way through the dense, yelling crowd that resisted even the flailings of Nehru himself, who sometimes tried to take command of the situation by jumping out of the car in which he was riding with Eisenhower. In another open car farther back in the procession Ann and Goodpaster were all but afloat in tossed flowers. Although it was dark, both of them had donned sunglasses to avoid being struck in the eyes by cascades of marigolds. Toward the end, the police finally sprang the president's car loose from the multitude and sped him to the Rashtrapati Bhavan, where he jumped into a hot bath and dressed according to his mood. Aglow over the welcome accorded the first American president ever to visit India, he invited his staff to join him in his suite for drinks and dinner on the same day that they had breakfasted in Pakistan and lunched in Afghanistan. "The president's cheeks were pink and rosy, and he was wearing a black tie," Ann recalled. "I came in bedraggled, along with the others."

Two aspects of living in the Rashtrapati Bhavan affected her. One was that sleeping a bit late was out of the question, because early in the morning a military band struck up a lively march in the courtyard. The other was that the marble stairs were so slippery that when Ann went to see the president on the floor below hers, she carried her high-heeled shoes and padded down in her stocking feet to keep from falling.

On the second day in New Delhi she was in Parliament to hear him speak. In the White House she had once sat in the Oval Office when he talked about Nehru. She quoted Eisenhower:

> "The fellow is a strange mixture, intellectually arrogant and of course at the same time suffering from an inferiority complex . . . schizophrenia."
>
> President said he had one real talk with him, one afternoon and evening, listened to him carefully, argued with him some. (When Columbia gave Nehru an honorary degree.) He was wholly unaware of our general trend of thinking, just as we maybe are unaware of their thinking.

After the speech in Parliament, the president introduced Ann to Nehru. She found him not unfriendly but cold and businesslike.

From India, Eisenhower turned homeward, with six stops still ahead of him, the first being Teheran for several hours. The road in from Mehrabad Airport was dotted with bands, all, it seemed, playing the same tune, "The Colonel Bogie March," recently popularized by the movie *The Bridge on the River Kwai*. A feature of the welcome that really shocked the American visitors was the covering of the road for at least a solid mile with Persian rugs. As the heavy press buses rolled over them, the passengers felt almost like vandals. At the royal palace the president had lunch and a long talk with Shah Mohammad Reza

Pahlavi. Ann was invited to lunch with a group of Iranian diplomats. She felt cold and rumpled from traveling and had not had a manicure in weeks. She noticed that her hosts followed the custom of kissing a woman's hand. Mortified, she held out her hand with the fingers doubled back at the knuckles, so that the diplomats were practically kissing her fist. At luncheon she expressed some dismay at the apparent squandering of Persian rugs under the wheels of the motorcade. It was very good for the rugs, she was assured. "That is not the way we treat them in America," she said.

The next stop was Athens at the weary end of a day that had begun in India. At first Athens went badly for Ann. The combination of an incomplete presidential speech text and missing typewriters put her in what she said were hysterics. But the next day, as scheduled, Eisenhower boarded the cruiser *Des Moines* for a journey across the Mediterranean to Tunis and then north to Toulon on the French coast. Because naval ships were off-limits to female passengers, Ann, after a tour of the Acropolis, flew to Paris. From there she took an overnight train to Toulon to rejoin Eisenhower for a day-long return to the French capital on a sumptuously appointed special train. Still working on acknowledgment of gifts, she wrote to Ralph H. Graner, an officer at the American embassy in New Delhi, who had been assigned to help her with the task.

En Route Toulon to Paris
December 18, 1959

Dear Ralph:

This is Presidential stationery (which is a crime to use)—but I am trapped between the President's bedroom and a conference and can't move.

I don't know whether I asked you to acknowledge for us a replica of a spinning wheel kit. The slip accompanying it is attached. Will you handle it, unless you think the member of the Planning Commission should have a Presidential letter?

More later. Meantime am exhausted.

Sincerely,
Ann C. Whitman

After spending three days in Paris in talks with de Gaulle, Adenauer, and Macmillan, Eisenhower flew to Madrid. The state dinner that night was at the Oriente Palace. Ann was invited. She managed to get her letters finished in time, only to be devastated by bureaucratic mistakes. The State Department notified her that information she had been given to include in the letters was erroneous. They had to be rewritten. "No state dinner," she recalled laconically.

The next day, December 22, the last of the trip, Eisenhower breakfasted with Generalissimo Francisco Franco at the Prado Palace. In midday the president was in Casablanca, conferring with King Mohamed V of Morocco after a picturesque welcome by rifle-bearing Berber tribesmen. "We've come to see the sultan of America," one of them said. That night Eisenhower ended the goodwill journey at Andrews Air Force Base, near Washington, after another "routine" three-continent day. The trip had been a marvel of logistics and precise movement, an achievement captured by the laconic judgment pronounced by Eisenhower's speechwriter, Kevin McCann. McCann, who returned to Washington wearing a fez, the image of an Irish sultan, said: "I don't know how many friends we made today for the United States; in fact, we may have lost a few. But, by God, we kept the schedule!"

■ 12 ■

On January 20, 1960, Eisenhower began the final year of his term and spoke to Ann about the future. He said he was contemplating writing his memoirs after he retired and might establish an office in Gettysburg. He asked her whether in that event she would be willing to remain with him, at least long enough to get it well organized.

"I said I would do anything he wanted me to do," she recorded. "He said that he had thought that while I was willing to sacrifice my life for the country for eight years, he didn't think I would want to when he was a private citizen. I said that was the silliest thing he had ever said, that my dedication to him was ten times my dedication to my country. He admitted that might be so."

The last year in the White House was not the happiest one for either of them. The president was irritable a good deal of the time, and Ann had spells of discouragement about work.

The third of the major international goodwill tours, this one to South America, began on February 22, with an overnight stay in San Juan, Puerto Rico. In the ensuing days, hectic ones for Ann, Eisenhower addressed parliaments in Brazil, Argentina, Chile, and Uruguay. Everywhere he went, large and friendly crowds greeted him.

The first stop in South America was Brasilía, the modern capital rising in the remote interior of Brazil. Ann's bedroom in the Alvaredo Palace was on the same floor as those of the president and Milton Eisenhower, who was on the trip as an authority on Latin America. Unlike the night in Madrid, she was not invited to the state dinner; in a not very cheerful mood she spent the evening working in her room. Unable to speak Portuguese, she did not call room service but settled for a peppermint patty and two sleeping pills. "I felt abandoned," she recalled. "As I was getting dopey, there was a lot of knocking on the door. I knew who it was, but I was mad at the world and called, 'Go away—I want to sleep' " On the receiving end of an order for a change, General Eisenhower retreated with his brother, presumably in good order. From Brasilía the journey took the president to Rio de Janeiro, and then, on February 25, he flew on a side trip to São Paulo to spend several hours. Then he reboarded *Air Force One* for the return flight with President Juscelino Kubitschek, for whom he was to hold a reception in Rio that evening. Before takeoff, Eisenhower received a stark message.

A short time earlier, people who happened to be on the Rio waterfront looking out over the dense clouds that shrouded Sugar Loaf Mountain saw a gruesome sight. Objects were falling out of the clouds into the harbor. Some appeared to be human forms. Others were unmistakably airplane wings and fuselages. A United States navy transport flying in from Buenos Aires had collided with a two-engine Brazilian airliner. Aboard the four-engine navy plane were nineteen members of the United States Navy Band, who were arriving to play at Eisenhower's reception that evening. Altogether there were thirty-eight naval personnel, including the crew, aboard the transport. Only three survived. Twenty-two people aboard the Real Airlines plane perished. The president "feels terrible," Hagerty told reporters. The reception was canceled, as Eisenhower went to Miguel Conto Hospital to comfort the survivors. The band had not made the trip from the United States merely for the reception. It had been in South America for several days of engagements and had planned to top off the tour by playing for the president in Rio.

After the hospital, Eisenhower repaired to the American embassy residence, where Ann was waiting to do whatever she could. "President Eisenhower seemed so upset after what had happened," recalled Alice Boyce, a member of the White House staff working with Ann. "Ann seemed to know just what to do to console him—who to call, what to say." Ambling about the ambassador's study, Eisenhower's mood was not improved by the sight of a photograph of Truman on a wall.

Nothing in Ann's life in those years, it seemed, happened without letters being involved somehow. She and Alice had written about thirty of them, thanking mayors, police chiefs, and others along the route who had been involved in facilitating the trip. The letters were ready to be mailed. After the president retired, a waiter brought in some drinks for the two women and for Wiley T. Buchanan, Jr., then the State Department's protocol chief, who was with them. While the three were relaxing, Alice accidentally knocked a bourbon highball over the whole pile of letters. Buchanan sprang into action and fetched some rope or twine, which he strung across the room for the secretaries to dry them on. It looked like washday at the embassy. The dampness, however, left a mark on the president's pale-green stationery. Ann coolly declared that all the letters had to be retyped. When she returned to Washington, she wrote to Graner, her friend at the embassy in New Delhi:

> We survived the South American trip, but barely. This time the people who handled the baggage devised a new torture. I rarely got to the hotel before 12 o'clock in the evening; rule was that all baggage had to be picked up before 11 o'clock the night before we left any place. You can imagine the net result.

An entry in her diary, not attributed to any particular event, makes for interesting reading in light of White House attacks on news coverage in recent years when the scene, but not necessarily the professional reporting, has been dominated by television. She wrote:

> *In talking with Jim Hagerty the President suggested that Jim, who is going to appear before some panel of ASNE [the American Society of Newspaper Editors], make a point of saying how well the newspaper people with him on trips had behaved—how much they had impressed the press of other countries and on how he, the President, believed they had influenced that press.*

In March 1960 Prime Minister Macmillan was in Washington, and Eisenhower transferred their talks to Camp David. The two of them, of course, stayed in Aspen, the main lodge. Ann and Macmillan's confidential secretary occupied Laurel, a nearby two-bedroom cottage. In the morning when Ann dressed and looked out, she saw the prime minister walking about by himself. She opened the door and bade him good morning and inquired whether she could do anything for him. He replied that he was looking for his secretary. Rain was falling, and Ann urged him to take a shortcut through her unmade bedroom. The rest of the story she related in a letter to friends.

"Later in the afternoon I was with the President when he and Macmillan were having a drink. The President, who had forgotten that he had introduced me to Macmillan at Geneva, started the introduction all over again. The Prime Minister said, 'Oh, but I was in Mrs. Whitman's bedroom this morning.' The President came back, 'Well, that's nice work if you can get it!' "

On May 5 Ann became entangled in one of those exquisite White House contretemps the press never learns about. When she arrived at work early, she found her small office crowded with the president, General Persons, Gordon Gray, then special assistant to the president for national security affairs, and others. After a week of civil defense tests, a secret plan had just been put into effect for a mock emergency meeting of the National Security Council to be held as soon as possible at the secret underground Relocation Center at High Point, North Carolina. Helicopters had already taken off from the Pentagon to the

White House and other designated points to pick up the president and other NSC members and staff.

As Ann arrived, Gray's secretary was telephoning from another office to alert the high officials to the mock emergency and direct them to where they were to board their helicopters. General Nathan F. Twining, chairman of the Joint Chiefs of Staff, somehow never arrived at his helicopter. Mrs. Thomas S. Gates, wife of the then secretary of defense, dashed to the family car in her nightgown and sped the secretary to his appointed spot. Armed guards who did not recognize him demanded to see his pass. He discovered he had left it home. At first the guards would not allow him to pass, but in a presumably frantic scene he finally convinced them of his identity. Budget Director Stans's car would not start, but Allen W. Dulles, director of central intelligence, whisked by and picked him up. When Gray's secretary called Dr. George B. Kistiakowsky, the president's science adviser, he said to call back in ten minutes. He was shaving. But he was supposed to be in his helicopter in ten minutes, the secretary protested. Although Secretary Gates took off in the nick of time, his NSC book was delivered to the White House by mistake. When Ann had a chance to look up, she saw Samuel Mitchell, an attendant, wandering through the corridors in some bewilderment as to what to do with it.

Eisenhower got off in his helicopter from the South Lawn just in time to miss the news of a true emergency. Hagerty, who had remained in the White House, was notified that Khrushchev had announced the shooting down of a United States U-2 reconnaissance plane over the Soviet Union. The press secretary sent word to Goodpaster in High Point to inform the president.

"Jim was furious," Ann noted in her diary, "because an hour later he had not heard from General Goodpaster and found out that General Goodpaster had not even informed the president."

Considering that the downing of the U-2, piloted by Francis Gary Powers, was one of the disasters of the Eisenhower administration, reversing an early movement toward Soviet-American détente, Hagerty's fury was perhaps understandable. He slumped in Ann's office like a man watching the approaching end of the world. Because of long experiences with Hagerty's moods, Ann could not have been surprised. Some others might have been. Hagerty was a formidable official in the Eisenhower White House. Even today, long after his death, he is rightly assigned an important role in the growing history of relations between the White House on one side and the press—newspapers, magazines, and television—on the other. No other White House press secretary has ever matched Hagerty's macho. The Ann Whitman diaries, however, reveal another side. Unbeknownst to reporters at the White House certainly, he spent a good deal of time in Ann's office unburdening himself of his frustrations and angers. "Whenever someone in the administration did something that caused embarrassment," she recalled years later, "Jim would come in and air his complaints to me, and he always had the same remedy to suggest: ship him to Alaska."

Her diary cites numerous instances of Hagerty's visits:

June 15, 1957
A State Department leak. All this and other things had Jim Hagerty talking to himself.

August 18, 1958
Jim Hagerty very upset at the composition of [United States] delegates to UNESCO—a "third-rate group" . . . [he feels] that the President is not getting proper advice on appointments.

[March 1960]
A group from State and Defense came in to consider problem of high altitude flying over Berlin. . . . Later Jim Hagerty was in a fury because the announcement was made by Herter in such a way as not to give the real reason for the decision, but to leave the impression that the President was "giving in" to Khrushchev and to our allies.

October 4, 1960
The President's breakfast guest was Paul-Henri Spaak [secretary general of NATO]. . . . Jim Hagerty was in his usual state of wrath when anything is done that he is not consulted on—this time his pitch was that having a meeting with the head of NATO would antagonize the heads of government at the UN General Assembly.

The U-2 controversy boiled on. After another NSC meeting on May 9 Eisenhower said to Ann, "I would like to resign." He "seemed very depressed in the morning," she noted, "but by afternoon had bounced back with his characteristic ability to accept bad news, not dwell on it, and so go ahead. . . . Later the President practiced golf shots. . . ."

In several more days Ann was back in Paris with the president for a long-scheduled and dramatic Big Four summit meeting. Khrushchev had visited Eisenhower in Washington in the fall of 1959. Khrushchev reciprocated by inviting the president to visit the Soviet Union in the summer of 1960. Now the trip hung in the balance because of the U-2 affair. If he had chosen to do so, Khrushchev might have reacted to the incident temperately. Instead he arrived in Paris with clenched teeth, causing suspicion that he might use the U-2 affair to torpedo the summit conference. That is exactly what he proceeded to do. And to top it off, he bluntly disinvited Eisenhower. The president was enraged.

"The past weeks, two I guess," Ann wrote to Marie McCrum after the return to Washington, "have been incredible and my own reaction has been unbelief, daze. Paris was a nightmare—just a nightmare of waiting, occasionally typing a page, not knowing when you would be needed and not knowing what to do to go ahead on your own. I had, surprisingly, a small piece of social life and got taken out to three very nice and one not so nice restaurant, at all hours of course. (Usually I eat a sandwich in the Crillon Bar). But other than that I subsisted on my usual watercress sandwiches."

The last of the four major Eisenhower trips was one to the Far East in June 1960. Just as one incident had dominated the South American trip, however, so another incident knocked off what was supposed to have been the capstone of the Asian tour, namely, a visit to Japan. While in Manila, the president learned that the Japanese government had canceled it because of anti-American riots. Consequently, the trip, in which he also visited the Philippines, Okinawa, Taiwan, and South Korea, was truncated and confused. There were big crowds welcoming him, especially in Seoul, but no real motif for the journey as the Japanese climax was lacking. With no place else to go then, Eisenhower flew back to Hawaii for several days of golf. It was a big moment of sorts for Ann. She and the staff were quartered in the marine barracks. For the first time, she was given authority to order her own helicopter. And off she went, soaring over Honolulu!

After the dismal events at the Paris summit Ann detected a change in Eisenhower's mood, as she commented in her diary. "The President has spent two weekends at the farm, and one weekend at West Point. He has been, almost without exception, in a bad humor—with me, that is—but on the surface has managed to hold his temper and control his emotions far better than I even thought he could." At the same time a dichotomy had developed between some journalists' perception of Eisenhower after the departure of Dulles and Adams and Ann's perception of presidential grumpiness. A wave of news stories and commentaries hailed a "new" Eisenhower, a president suddenly, energetically, and happily seizing the reins in his own hands after supposedly having delegated considerable areas of authority to Adams and Dulles. Ann, however, disavowed the theory of a "new" and an "old" Eisenhower. Critically, she endorsed the position that the press had long underestimated Eisenhower's leadership and was now compensating by depicting a "new" Eisenhower. "Scotty Reston of all people," she said in her diary, "hit the nail closer to the head than anyone when he derided the [idea of a] 'new' Eisenhower and said that the President was acting freer, more sure of himself, than at any time since the war days."

On the other hand, she found changes at work, with some consequences for herself. General Persons was a much more relaxed chief of staff than Adams and hence the staff was more relaxed. It was Ann's view that under Persons Eisenhower was brought into the discussion of problems earlier and before conclusions had been reached. Thus she saw him leading the staff to ultimate decisions. With the stricter Adams regime relaxed, more of the staff had ready access to the president and, consequently, Ann had somewhat less. Also the staff had been enlarged by the appointment of John Eisenhower as an assistant to Goodpaster. But not even John was impervious to his father's testiness. When he had a question for the president, he sometimes found it safer to have Ann go in and ask it.

As far back as mid-August 1959 Ann had wondered whether, with the changing order, she should resign. "But," she added in her diary, "I don't want to, and I don't want to certainly while I still feel that the President has any shred of affection for me or feels that I can in any way serve him better than someone new." It was after that that he asked her if she would remain with him at least for a time when he had retired. After the bitterness in Paris and the embarrassment of Eisenhower's being turned back almost on the doorstep of Japan, the summer of 1960 in Washington and Newport was not easy for Ann. Eisenhower struck her as being angry at events, as having a "very 'mad' look on his face," as she noted in her diary of July 13, 1960. Among other things, he was soured by such developments as the rise of Fidel Castro, the nationalistic uprisings in the Congo, and the prospective nomination of John F. Kennedy by the Democrats. Reflecting twenty-six years later on the president's mood in the summer of 1960, Ann said, "He was sorry at giving up the presidency." For a time at Newport she did not see him much because he shunned the office. But there were exceptions.

"One evening," she wrote in her diary of the thirteenth at Newport, "he suggested I meet him on the boat and we did have a fine time for an hour and a half—he signed everything up and was comparatively cheerful, which is rare these days."

At that time, too, she was so amused by what she called the saga of a salmon caught in the Moisie River in East Quebec by Pete Jones of Cities Service that she recorded it in her diary.

"The President talked to Mrs. Jones and decided it was the one thing he wanted for Mrs. George Allen's dinner Friday (she is a Catholic). Mr. Jones had this particular salmon driven to Floyd Bennet Field, New York; the Navy had a pilot pick it up and deliver it to the President's quarters. (Probably by helicopter.) It was discovered the oven at Fort Adams [a nearby facility at Newport] was too small and the fish was helicoptered to the Officers Club at Coaster's Island, cooked, and delivered back to Fort Adams for, presumably, a delicious dinner."

If Franklin Delano Roosevelt had ordered such consumption of naval aviation gasoline for delivering a fish for a dinner party, the Republican national chairman would have gone on radio, claiming the extravagance with taxpayers' money was ultimate proof that Roosevelt had never had to meet a payroll.

Back in Washington again, Eisenhower faced other problems. "The President again in office early," Ann noted in her diary of August 19, 1960, "this time worrying about where his portrait is going to hang in the White House."

As the Kennedy-Nixon campaign was getting started, she jotted this entry on August 30:

"The President . . . visited Vice President Nixon in the hospital, who was there for knee. He managed to get an infected knee, which had the possibilities of serious trouble. However, it seems that everything will be all right. . . .

"Later the President intimated that while the Vice President was 'all right' when he visited the hospital, there was some lack of warmth. He mentioned again, as he has several times, the fact that the Vice President has very few friends. Of course the difference to me is obvious . . . for whatever it is worth—the President is a man of integrity and sincere in his every action, be it possibly wrong. He radiates this, everybody knows it, everybody trusts and loves him. But the Vice President sometimes seems like a man who is acting like a nice man rather than being one."

Eisenhower spoke at the United Nations General Assembly session in New York on September 22, 1960. Khrushchev also was there, playing up to Castro, who was the biggest show in town that season. Only a year before had Eisenhower made history by entertaining the Soviet premier in Washington. Ann had been involved merely peripherally. "The President's only comment to me after his long meeting with Mr. Khrushchev in his office," she had written in her diary of September 16, 1959, "was . . . 'those sweet words—but he won't change his mind about anything.' " Eisenhower spoke to Ann on the subject again after a dinner at the Soviet embassy during the Khrushchev visit. "The President said," she recorded, "that the Chairman had accused him of being able by a 'wink' to determine the kind of reception that the people would accord Mr. Khrushchev; the President had tried to get across to him how utterly impossible such a thing was."

Ann was in the audience at the United Nations when Eisenhower spoke. "Very impressive," she noted. "Sat next to Bulgarians and they sat on their hands. Man next to me burped and yawned constantly through the President's speech. I could only see the back of Mr. K's head. . . . Atmosphere of UN tense, atmosphere of New York charged."

A few days later the president spoke to Ann again about Khrushchev, using the most improbable terms. She wrote:

"The other night, talking about Mr. K and his threats, the President told me what [the British diplomat] Lord Home said, with sarcasm, that sometimes he wished 'the world could go back to the old methods of diplomacy' . . . meaning of course the big stick. The President strongly intimated that he wished there was no moral restriction that prevented him from one night pushing the proper button and sending all of our atomic bombs in the direction of the Communist block. This is the strongest statement I have ever heard him make on the subject."

As the end of the Eisenhower administration was approaching, public interest centered on the campaign. The president and those around him were disappointed by Nixon's performance, especially in the televised debates, which Eisenhower had warned him to avoid. Kennedy won and monopolized attention. Eisenhower went to Augusta for the last time as president, and his friends, as Ann wrote to Whit, besieged her with job offers.

Douglas Black of Doubleday & Company "said that if I didn't go with the President I should go with him." Bennett Cerf, president of Random House, "had previously said come to them." Vernon B. Stauffer, chairman of Litton Industries, Food Services Group, and chairman of the board of the Cleveland Indians, "wants me to go back to Cleveland (that I turned down flat!!!)." But Pete Jones, "who is my anchor to windward, says I must not 'run out on the President,' a view I guess is shared by a lot of the President's friends."

The future was unsettled. Ann felt that she and Whit had grown apart. She knew of his continuing friendship with Sigrid Taillon. Ann and Whit were still married, however, and evidently he had said nothing to change that. "I truly thought we could make our marriage work," she said years later. "Whit certainly reveled in the contacts I made, and made for him, using them, as I have since been told, quite freely."

On the snowy night before the Kennedy inauguration, Ann, Mary Caffrey, Tom Stephens, and Kevin McCann held what Ann later described as a combined celebration and wake at a restaurant on Seventeenth Street. Almost intimidated by the weather, they lingered for hours over drinks. When they finally emerged, no cab was to be seen in the deep snow. Suddenly either Stephens or McCann proclaimed, "We're still in power!" One of them telephoned the White House, and an official car was dispatched to take them home.

Feeling more than mildly ill from one of the worst hangovers she ever had, Ann wrote later, she "sloshed and skidded" on foot down Sixteenth Street on January 20, 1961, to go to work on her boss's last half-day in office. She was proud that day, she continued, "of what I thought . . . was an achievement by the President and his staff of eight mainly prosperous years for our country." She recalled that early in the administration Gabriel Hauge had given the president a plaque for his desk, inscribed with words attributed to Claudio Aquaviva: *Suaviter in modo fortiter in re* [Gently in manner, strongly in deed]. "That says precisely how he performed," Ann wrote.

*　　*　　*

In New York shortly after the Kennedy inauguration, Ann and Whit quarreled. Soon he went to Mexico and got a divorce. He and Sigrid were married on December 23, 1961. For Ann, the pain was deep, beyond anything the ensuing years could cure. Naturally, she reflected on Adele Levy's admonition to her in 1952 that acceptance of the White House job might undermine her marriage.

"Of course, Mrs. Levy was so, so right," Ann wrote in a letter to Marie Clancy on December 27, 1961. "And yet I don't know what else, under the circumstances, anyone could have done. If I had not gone to Washington, I would have regretted it for the rest of my life."

In early 1961 she accepted Eisenhower's offer of a job as his personal secretary in retirement, starting to work in Gettysburg in May. She did so because she wanted to remain with him and because she no longer had a home that meant anything to her. For all that she had come to dread Gettysburg during the administration, she now found it even worse. The first three weeks seemed like three years. Outside her work, the town offered Ann little, if anything, to interest or cheer her. In time, she began to fear that loneliness would consume her. With little else to do, she recalled, she drank too much. She lived at the old Gettysburg Hotel, which was drab above the first floor. Every night she had the same thing for dinner: four martinis, a hamburger, and slices of tomato. Bryce Harlow, who came to town occasionally to consult with the former president on his memoirs, remarked afterward: "Ann worshipped Ike. She would step off the world for him. She did by going to Gettysburg after the White House."

Relief came in December 1961 when she went with the Eisenhowers to California for the winter. General and Mrs. Eisenhower stayed in a house at the Dorado Country Club in Palm Desert. He had an office at the ranch of his friends Jacqueline Cochran and her husband, Floyd B. Odlum, near Indio, about ten miles away. Ann also had a cottage there. She remembers having one of her best times in California. She liked Jacqueline Cochran. On occasion, with Jacqueline piloting, they would fly to Las Vegas in the latter's plane for a couple of days at the slot machines and gambling tables. To Ann's pleasure, the ranch often swarmed with guests, including Bob Hope and other movie stars. She enjoyed the scenery. "I love . . . the mountains which change color every hour of the day," she once wrote to Marie Clancy. Ann recalled seeing little of Mrs. Eisenhower.

"I saw the president once a day," she said. "I used to go over in the morning between seven-forty-five and eight-thirty to take dictation. I hated it. I tried to keep out of Mrs. Eisenhower's way. It was clear that she did not want me around."

Mrs. Eisenhower's attitude, which evidently had persisted from the time of the 1952 campaign when she tried to get Ann removed as the general's secretary, was one of two main reasons for Ann's decision to leave Gettysburg and Eisenhower's employ. The atmosphere of loneliness had become intolerable. So had Mrs. Eisenhower's attitude.

"I am terribly sad about leaving DDE," she told Mrs. Clancy in the letter of December 27, 1961, "but I must for several reasons, but the one I am sticking to is the Gettysburg atmosphere."

Curiously, sometime after Ann told Eisenhower she was leaving, she had second thoughts about it. But by then he had engaged another secretary. Unceremoniously, Ann returned to New York.

◼ 13 ◼

One day in the late 1930s or early 1940s, while Ann was working at her desk in the Levys' Park Avenue apartment, she heard Mrs. Levy talking to a visitor. Glancing up, Ann saw, framed in a doorway, a man about her own age, a stocky, strongly built man with an easy bearing, a large head crowned by wavy brown hair, and a broad face with narrow eyes commanding quick changes of expression. Adele Levy introduced him to Ann as Nelson Rockefeller. Then, called to the telephone, she asked Ann, who was then in her early thirties, to show him around the apartment. "He was very handsome and very nice," she recalled later. Rockefeller was interested in Mrs. Levy's paintings. Then president of the Museum of Modern Art, he had come to ask her to bequeath her collection to it. (Adele Levy bequeathed part of the collection to the museum, but left other paintings to galleries in different parts of the country for the pleasure of a wider range of viewers.) After the first visit, Ann saw Rockefeller two or three other times in the apartment. "On those visits," she remembered, "Nelson was friendly, dashing. When he wanted to be, he was a great charmer."

In January 1953 the two met again, this time in the White House. "We seemed to be just good friends from the start," she said later. Eisenhower had appointed Rockefeller to an advisory committee on government organization. Among other reforms, the group drew up plans for transforming the Federal Security Agency into the Department of Health, Education, and Welfare. Mrs. Oveta Culp Hobby, a Houston newspaper publisher and wartime head of the Women's Army Corps, became its first secretary and Rockefeller under secretary. Then, in December 1954, he replaced C. D. Jackson as special assistant to the president for psychological warfare, a post he held until the fall of 1955. For two and a half years, therefore, Nelson, as she called him, and Ann or mostly Annie, as he called her, continued to see each other often. When he had an appointment with the president, he would usually drop by her office for a chat, occasionally bringing her a small gift. "Since we were both from New York, he came to look upon me as an ally," she recalled. In minor ways, he took advantage of the "Ann Whitman end run."

"He was a great one," she said, "for ordering memorandums and public opinion surveys. He wanted the president to see them, but was afraid they would never reach him if they were sent through Goodpaster or Adams. So he would give them to me to give to the president at my discretion, and I did."

Rockefeller invited Ann to small dinners at his Washington residence on Foxhall Road. His marriage to his first wife, Mary Todhunter Clark Rockefeller, was foundering, and she was not present on such occasions. A few times Ann and Nelson dined alone together in a small library in the Foxhall house. He always drove her home afterward in a dilapidated car.

A guest one night was Robert Justus Kleberg, Jr., president of King Ranch, Inc., in Texas and son-in-law of the ranch's founder. Celebrated for its vastness, it encompassed all or parts of seven counties.

"The subject of the plight of blacks came up," Ann remembered, "and Bob Kleberg joined the discussion. I made a very brash remark about why they didn't do something about it at the King Ranch. It didn't set very well."

From the White House, Ann followed Rockefeller's widening political ambitions with interest. In her diary of October 18, 1957, she noted:

Nelson Rockefeller in, to talk to the President about his running for Governor of New York State. The President indicated he would like to see Nelson do this (he told me later that he wanted to see some fresh faces in the political picture) and suggested that Nelson talk closely with Tom Stephens regarding the possibility.

In his early years in office, Ann recalled, Eisenhower treated Rockefeller "like one of the smart young boys in the administration." He thought Rockefeller played a useful role as an adviser on psychological warfare.

"The President told me," she said afterward, "that out of a hundred ideas, Rockefeller might have one really bright one and thus it was worth having him around. The one bright idea was worth the ninety-nine that weren't."

In her diary of October 10, 1955, she quoted Eisenhower's astute comment about Rockefeller, who was famous for surrounding himself at great cost with brilliant thinkers and planners. (Dr. Henry A. Kissinger was the most conspicuous one.)

President said he did not think Nelson was perfect in his job because he was too used to borrowing brains instead of using his own. . . .

In 1958 the Republican party in New York nominated Rockefeller as its candidate for governor. Writing to Marie Clancy from the White House two months before the election, Ann wrote: "I desperately hope Nelson Rockefeller will win. (I am awfully fond of him.)" He won. When he became governor, Ann did what she could to keep him and Eisenhower in touch with each other. In certain disputes, she held Rockefeller's side of a case before the president. As Rockefeller jockeyed for the Republican presidential nomination in 1960, his relationship with Vice-President Nixon, the leading contender for it, was edgy. An example of this materialized on the eve of Khrushchev's visit to the United States, which aroused some opposition in the country, especially in certain conservative Catholic circles. Ann sent a note to Eisenhower:

August 14, 1959

Mr. President:

Rose Woods [Nixon's personal secretary] called me at the Vice President's urgent request (he had called her from Chicago) to say the following.

They have had several reports, the last one from a "totally unimpeachable source," that Nelson Rockefeller is being very critical of the Khrushchev visit. He is saying, according to this source, that the "Vice President is totally responsible for the visit" and that he, Rockefeller, "will stay away unless ordered not to do so by the President or the State Department."

She said—reflecting the Vice President—that it was terrible to make a political football of such an important thing connected with our foreign relations.

I said it just didn't sound like Nelson at all and that, after all, you had publicly stated that the decision to invite Khrushchev was yours alone and was made before the Vice President went to Russia. She knows that, but insists that Nelson is trying to make the visit a political issue. . . .

I have read in the paper a couple of comments that led me to suspect Nelson was trying to woo the anti-visit elements. One was a specific thing: that Nelson did not answer the invitation of the Soviet government to visit the exhibition at the Coliseum [in New York City] . . . .

a.

Nevertheless, whatever small things Ann might do to keep Rockefeller's relations with Eisenhower in good repair were being continually undone by Rockefeller. Strange as it may seem in view of Eisenhower's enormous popularity, an idea took hold in his second term, especially among aggressive younger politicians, that the president would be a drag on other Republicans running for office. To a large extent, this phenomenon was due to the impact on American opinion of the Soviet feat of launching *Sputnik* in 1957. Politicians and the press widely regarded that first leap into space as a sign that the Eisenhower administration had been outmaneuvered, with potentially great harm to the security of the United States. To Eisenhower's disgust, Rockefeller was one of the Republican presidential aspirants who shared the view that the administration's national security policies were not adequate to the Soviet challenges and thus were a liability to the party. In her diary Ann noted:

> February 17, 1959
> *The President is more than aware that he is considered a liability in some states—witness the way Rockefeller tried to keep him out [of the New York gubernatorial campaign last] year.*

As the Republican National Convention approached in 1960, Rockefeller—carelessly, in Ann's opinion—surprised and angered Eisenhower by publicly proposing a $3.5 billion increase in defense spending. Ann was busy on the telephone the next day, as a note in her diary shows:

> June 9, 1960
>
> Mr. President:
>
> Nelson Rockefeller called, twice to be exact. The last time he specifically asked to talk to you.
>
> His problem: He does not know whether or not in the best interests of the Republican Party (and he insists he is not hostile to the Party—that he is doing only what he thinks is best for the Party) he should become an avowed candidate. (He said he didn't think he would have any delegates, if he did). He repeated several times that his statement of yesterday did not criticize your Administration, but rather he was criticizing lack of leadership on the Vice President's part, in promulgating a program for the future, changing needs of our country.
>
> The first time he called I said I did not think he properly should ask you the question, that the decision was one that he should make on his own. Then, as I say, he called back to see if he could "chat" with you about it. I told him, you would be unavailable all afternoon and busy this evening—and the best I could do was to get this note to you at six o'clock. I did not promise to call him back tonight.
>
> a.

Eisenhower returned the calls two days later. Alluding to Rockefeller's sputtering moves toward becoming a presidential candidate, the president said that the governor was in danger of resembling "off again, on again, gone again Finnegan." Eisenhower added that anyone who wanted the Republican nomination "would have to get some kind of blessing from the President. He said therefore he hoped that the reasoned and positive approach [on defense spending which] he had advocated would be adopted by Nelson (instead of jumping on everybody)." Nixon, of course, was nominated without any threat from Rockefeller.

Sometime after leaving Eisenhower at the end of 1961, Ann worked briefly for Republican Citizens, an organization in Washington that had been formed to broaden and liberalize the Republican party and which Eisenhower actively supported. Then she returned to Manhattan and went to work for George L. Hinman, Republican national committeeman from New York and one of Rockefeller's foremost political advisers. As she had sensed, this proved to be an interim job before she was appointed to the governor's staff. Still disgusted with Rockefeller, Eisenhower was displeased. "What the president didn't understand," Ann said later, "was that I had to have a job—I needed the money." She also wrote: "I never asked for, or got, alimony. And I gave up willingly [almost] all assets [Whit and Ann] had acquired. [We] did have a brokerage account, and that we split."

Rockefeller, of course, had various secretaries in Albany, the state capital, and in New York, the two cities between which he divided his time. For the sake of continuity in his work he wanted one personal secretary who would travel back and forth with him on all occasions. He admired Ann and trusted her work. One day in the fall of 1964 he invited her to lunch in the RCA Building and asked her if she would be willing to take the traveling job, and she said she would. She was hired as of January 1, 1965. After Rockefeller arrived in Albany with his new secretary, later executive assistant, he grandly informed other members of the staff, "She ran the White House for Ike." Some read into his words a suggestion that she was about to run the governor's office for Rockefeller. Of course, Ann had never run the White House; Eisenhower had. Nor would she ever run the governor's office. Rockefeller would do that, incessantly. He wanted Ann for her reputation in the White House, her advice, her presence, her wide acquaintance with influential men and women, especially Republicans, her skill at correspondence, her executive talent, her ability to conserve a chief executive's time, and for the friendship and understanding that had grown between them. Now in his second term, he was still eyeing higher goals, and in that quest Ann could be an asset to him.

The change from Eisenhower to Rockefeller gave her a unique opportunity to compare working for the once-poor boy who had reached undreamed-of heights with working for the man of vast wealth and advantages who could never attain the heights of his dreams.

"The governor loved meetings," she said. "The president hated meetings. Nelson was always calling his staff into conference. I would become weary of sitting at a conference table. After a while it hurt. Try sitting in the same chair for five hours. I would get so tired of it I would wiggle. I was not alone in my restlessness. Once I was aghast when [Lieutenant Governor] Malcolm Wilson, who was sitting next to me, squirmed and knocked a large glass of orange juice from the table into his open briefcase on the floor beside his chair. When I looked down, I could see state documents swimming in juice.

"The governor worked hard or talked about his work all the time. It was difficult to get him to talk about anything else. The president was more sociable. He would talk to you about anything. The governor would take armsful of material home every night. Except for speech drafts and material, the president did not take work home. He preferred matters to be presented to him orally. Then he would give his answers and trust his subordinates to carry them out. The governor wanted almost everything submitted to him by subordinates in the form of memos. His idea was to get a paper written about something.

"Wherever he went he always carried with him two or three large red envelopes filled with papers. Staff people were encouraged to write memos, and the governor was very conscientious about bringing back in the morning answers to questions the staff had raised the night before. Unlike the president, he was terrible at dictating letters and speeches. He fragmented sentences. He used to explain to me with great pride how he could do not just one, but two or three, things at the same time. For instance, while talking on the phone, he could write something he had on his mind. He made a great virtue of this.

"The governor seldom went to the theater, the ballet, or the opera. I believe he played golf once a week with his brother Laurence at Pocantico Hills [the Rockefeller family estate in Westchester County]. The president played bridge at night with his friends, but not so the governor. He was too busy. As an executive he worked harder than the president, I guess, but he didn't have the inner confidence that the president had. The president decided things quickly and cleanly. He was the better administrator of the two.

"President Eisenhower was bright, masterful in the way he grasped situations. Sometimes you have to explain things repeatedly to people, not to him. The president would listen to argument, especially from Dulles. He thought Dulles had a better background on particular problems than he did. Governor Rockefeller didn't think anyone knew more than he did about the problems before him. The president was a skillful compromiser. He was not headstrong, but deliberate, patient. The governor made up his mind like a bulldozer and the hell with everybody. His strength was that he picked good people. On the whole, he may have had abler people around him than the president.

"Another thing, Nelson was way ahead of his time in the equal treatment of women. President Eisenhower did not believe a woman could do what a man could. Nelson promoted women all over the place. I felt he never hesitated to give me a man's job with a man's pay. In those days, talking about the sixties and seventies, women were making an issue of serving coffee in the office to men. Nelson used to get up and serve coffee to everybody.

"The president had a legion of friends. Nelson had no close friends. In earlier years, Jock Whitney, Bill Paley, and George Woods were pretty close to Nelson.* But the governor didn't have really close friends. His roommate at Dartmouth, John French, would call every year to invite him to the class luncheon, but that was the only time. Nelson never called him. In the corporate world the president had at least twenty-five good friends. Every one of them was a tycoon. When they came to Washington, they would call me, and often we could arrange a dinner. The president was delighted. But no friend called Nelson unless the friend wanted something. I tried to persuade him to give stag dinners, like the president's, but he never did. Nelson's chief interests were his work, his art, and his family. When he got involved in a big public problem, it was the problem that absorbed him, not having fun or seeing old friends. He loved his work and he lived it.

"The governor was not a snob. 'Hiya fella' pretty well typified him. He was a man with absolute lack of pretense. I felt I could say anything to him. He did not inspire awe, as the president did, although I quickly got over *that*. You would think a man like Rockefeller with all his wealth would scare you. And if he did set out to destroy someone, of course, he did a pretty good job. He was excessively friendly, if he wanted to be. But if he took a dislike to somebody, that person recognized it. As far as I was concerned, Nelson never, not once, consciously displayed wealth—it was just there. In the beginning, I was not unimpressed by the wealth and glamour surrounding him. After I got to know him, his money and position were things I never thought of. I was aware that he could make or break people, if so he chose, and sometimes he did.

"Certainly, he never spoke about his money. Yet I had a feeling that he thought he could do anything—could do some

* William S. Paley was chairman of the board of CBS. George Woods was chairman of the board of the First Boston Corporation and later chairman of the International Bank for Reconstruction and Development (World Bank).

things better than anyone else—because he was a Rockefeller."

Ann not only liked Rockefeller and generally found it enjoyable to work for him, but she also respected him for his diligence and accomplishments. Of course, working for a governor was not as exciting as working for a president. When she left the White House, she knew that any future job would be an anticlimax and prepared herself for it. For all the good side she saw of him, Rockefeller did not impress her as much or stir her admiration as deeply as Eisenhower had. She did not have to put as much of herself into working for him as she did for Eisenhower. Accordingly, she regretted that she could not do as much for the governor as she had done for the president. Because she had started from the beginning with Eisenhower, her large role with him was quickly carved out. In 1965, by contrast, she moved into an already strong and well-organized Rockefeller establishment. The work had been compartmentalized to a considerable extent. It was hard to change Rockefeller's way of doing things.

Nevertheless, Ann's impact on the governor's office was obvious.

"If Ann Whitman told you to do something, you did it," recalled Joseph W. Canzeri, a member of the staff, who handled advance work on Rockefeller's trips. "You'd assume the order came from the governor. She was the doorkeeper to Nelson Rockefeller's office."

James M. Cannon, a former senior editor of *Newsweek*, who was then special assistant to the governor, said, "Ann controlled Governor Rockefeller's appointments and his time: who got on the schedule and who didn't."

"She was always his eyes and ears," a colleague, Nancy Towel, remembered.

"People who knew the setup," said Hugh Morrow, a speechwriter and director of public relations for Rockefeller, "knew that if you wanted something done by the governor, you'd better get Ann on your side." He added: "Sometimes people were afraid of her. She could be mean as hell if she thought you were working against Nelson's interests."

"She could be very demanding," Cannon agreed. "Her voice would get rasping."

Joseph E. Persico, one of the governor's speechwriters and later the author of *The Imperial Rockefeller: A Biography of Nelson A. Rockefeller*, had a delightful lunch with Ann one noon in Albany. In midafternoon, she became angry with him on the telephone over some matter and hung up.

"It was a rare day," Mary McAniff Kresky of the Rockefeller staff said, "when she was not aware of the information that would go to the governor and when she herself had not put it in order. Daily, she usually set the priorities on what he should pay attention to."

Richard L. Dunham, the state budget director, recalled: "We perceived she had a big role with the governor. That's why we paid attention to her."

As Dunham, Cannon, Morrow, and others attest, gradually the feeling that it would be helpful to have Ann on one's side seeped into the offices in Albany, as it had years before into the White House. Even more so than in the White House, she was the confidante of the head man. Rockefeller talked to her frequently—in the office, at lunch, at dinner, on his airplane. His talk, she said, was almost entirely about office business, which inevitably included even the highest staff appointments and assignments. Rockefeller was surely one to make his own decisions, but who could say what weight her recommendations may have carried? "I can't imagine Rockefeller's taking Ann's opinion on a person in any but the most earnest way," Persico commented. "If Ann said, 'Yes, so-and-so is first rate,' that would weigh most heavily in the person's favor. Certainly more so than that of any other opinion Rockefeller would get."

Ann followed her old practice of writing letters for the governor's signature to people with whom she felt he should correspond. Later, after she had retired, he wrote to her in longhand, thanking her for, among other things, "all those superbly written letters which maintained for me contact with countless friends."

"I am also grateful," he said, "for all you did to help key staff members who, because of their respect for you, asked for and listened to your sound advice."

When he was still one of the youngest and most naïve members, Harry Albright on more than one occasion tried to get past Ann to see the governor to resign on the spot in anger and discouragement. First, she would insist, Albright must go out and walk around the block. He did—and never resigned. Years later, when he was president and chief executive officer of the Dime Savings Bank of New York, he said, "She saved people's asses time and again. . . . I consider her more influential in my life than anyone else except my wife."

"In my first few months as budget director," Richard Dunham said later, "I didn't think I would survive. Sometimes the phone would ring. It was the governor bawling me out and ordering me to come up and see him. I wouldn't know what was wrong and couldn't prepare any explanation or defense."

When Dunham would pass through Ann's office on the way to the governor's, she would hastily acquaint him with the problem and suggest what he should say to Rockefeller. Dunham, too, went on to a very successful career.

In his handwritten letter Rockefeller also thanked Ann for her "unfailing sensitive and perceptive advice that so often kept me from making mistakes." The impression among former members of his staff is that when he was governor, she advised him on many things, some of them pertaining to New York State affairs, and that he generally took her advice. Still, it was hard to read Rockefeller's mind. Joe Persico once asked Ann how a person of the governor's intelligence could sometimes seem most opaque. "It's deliberate—to keep you off balance," she replied. Sometimes Rockefeller did not want to hear advice that he surmised would be negative.

Mary Kresky recalled: "It was rare when the governor did not agree with Ann's advice, even though he did not always follow through. Sometimes when he was sure Ann would disagree, he did not ask her." On occasion, he would dismiss her advice with a smile. Working one day on a report that in his mind suddenly took precedence over everything else on his schedule, he asked Ann to inquire whether Lieutenant Governor Wilson could substitute for him in delivering a political speech upstate, to which Rockefeller had committed himself for the next day. Such a cancellation would have been abrupt indeed. "It will cost you," Ann admonished. He shrugged off the warning. Later she returned with word that Wilson could deliver the speech in his place. Rockefeller was pleased. "It will cost you," she repeated to no avail.

It was not uncommon for Rockefeller to assemble his staff to solicit advice after he had already made up his mind what he was going to do, regardless. In October 1972 he held a staff meeting in Pocantico Hills to discuss the program he intended to present to the legislature the following January. One surprising item was a bill mandating a life sentence for anyone convicted of trafficking in hard drugs. Rockefeller turned first to Ann. "What do you think of that?" he asked. "It may be a bit drastic," she replied. Rockefeller proposed the bill. It was passed and became law in 1973. In 1979, under Governor Hugh Carey, the law was modified. Because it was so severe, courts, prosecutors, and jurors were reluctant to enforce its provisions. As Ann had said six years earlier, the measure was a bit drastic.

By the time Ann went to work for Rockefeller, her life had changed a great deal. Even though, during the White House years, she and Whit had mostly lived apart, the divorce was hard on her. Gradually, however, the emptiness was filled to some extent by a warm and lasting relationship with C. Edmonds Allen, the genial vice-president for sales and director of special services for United Press International. Allen, who lived in Manhattan and had a country house in Mattituck, Long Island, was the best friend of Merriman Smith, who had introduced him to Ann during the Eisenhower period. The three of them occasionally had lunch or dinner together in Washington. A graduate of Washington and Lee University, Allen had once worked as a reporter for the *St. Louis Post-Dispatch*. At other times he had done some script writing in Hollywood and had worked for Lowell Thomas, a prominent lecturer, traveler, and radio commentator. Eventually he wound up in the commercial end of the news business. He was the father of three grown children, and his wife had died in 1963. He and Ann began going out together in New York in 1964. "Ed stabilized my life," she said years later.

Allen, who was a member of The Players, a theatrical club in Gramercy Park founded by Edwin Booth, loved the theater, and he and Ann went to plays. In winter, one of her favorite pastimes was going with him to Sunday afternoon showings of old motion pictures at The Players. Each week an actor or actress who had starred in the movie to be shown was invited to attend. Ann thus met such great figures of the cinema as Maurice Chevalier, James Cagney, and Joan Crawford, and renewed her acquaintanceship with Ralph Bellamy, whom she had met through Whit in the 1940s. In the summers, Ann and Ed often went to the country on weekends. Throughout their long friendship she spent a good deal of time at his place in Mattituck. Then, in 1980 and 1981, by which time Ann had retired, Ed's health was ruined by strokes. She remained a faithful companion. Nothing else took priority when he wanted her at his bedside.

Working for Rockefeller, Ann had to divide her time between Albany and New York because he did. Every week they shuttled back and forth between the two cities, flying up to Albany on Sunday or on Monday morning and flying down to New York on Wednesday or Thursday. Whatever the day or direction, for Ann each trip meant being loaded down with memorandums and reports, though she was not always as busy as she looked. Sometimes the diligence was just a sham. As Eisenhower had done, too, Rockefeller occasionally shuffled papers with Ann, merely feigning work to inhibit other passengers from bothering him.

Ann detested Albany. The streets were filled with slush and snow in winter. In those days, at least, the center of the city, which is where she spent her time, had an upstate shabbiness

about it. The bars and restaurants were hives full of politi
lobbyists, and reporters, all talking more or less on the
subject. Ann lived in the Wellington Hotel and could not be
"Every hotel room in Albany smelled of fifty years of
smoke," she said. Rockefeller heard enough complaints from
on the subject so that he invited her to move into the Execu
Mansion along with some other members of his so-called
eling staff, who had been living there. Several of the assista
Morrow and Cannon among them, also regularly traveled
tween New York and Albany with the governor, and for cor
nience he put them up in the mansion. "We were all part of
family," Ann recalled. "When the governor had nothing else
his schedule, we used to have dinner with him."

The domiciling of Ann in the mansion was too good
opportunity for her old prankster friend Tom Stephens to p
up. He also had gone to work for the New York State governme
after leaving the White House, although his office was in Ne
York City. He went to Albany frequently, however, and or
night, as he often did, he took Ann to dinner at the DeWi
Clinton Hotel. Afterward, he got her a taxicab, cautioning th
driver out of range of her hearing, "This lady gets hallucinations
Sometimes she thinks she lives with Rockefeller." As the cal
pulled away with Ann in the backseat, the driver asked her
destination. "The Executive Mansion," she said. He refused to
take her there. A hullabaloo ensued. Finally Ann got him to
drive her to the state police post outside the mansion. Still
indignant the next day, she related to Stephens the story of the
idiotic driver. It was some time before Stephens dared tell her
exactly what had happened.

The excitement of life at the top that had lured Ann to the
White House in 1952 was of a different order when working for
a governor. Still, there were sides to it that she relished. After
keeping her busy in New York one day when she had intended
to be traveling to Ed Allen's on Long Island, Rockefeller had her
flown to Mattituck in his helicopter to make up for lost time. She
often lunched with the governor and his political or business
friends in New York. She became a good friend of his new wife,

Happy, and not infrequently lunched with her or had an afternoon drink at the Rockefellers' duplex apartment at 812 Fifth Avenue. The governor gave frequent business dinners there somewhat in the guise of social affairs, and Ann was invited. Outside the office, she spent considerable time with the Rockefellers. One Labor Day weekend when he discovered that she was going to be alone in New York, the governor got her to join Happy and him at Pocantico Hills. Ann once accompanied them on a Caribbean vacation. At other times she worked with him on reports while at his summer home in Seal Harbor, Maine, and at his place on St. John's Island in the Virgin Islands. Once after she had been ill he insisted on sending her and her friend Mary Caffrey Stephens to spend a week at Laurence Rockefeller's house at Dorado Beach in Puerto Rico.

The governor took a keen interest in all his own houses, scattered from Seal Harbor to Venezuela, Ann said.

"He knew every piece of furniture in all of them," she commented. "He completely ran his domestic household. He bought the china, he arranged the guest list for parties, supervised the seating, the menu. Nothing was too small to catch his eye. I remember once, in Albany, arriving with him for an afternoon reception at the mansion, some five minutes before the guests (New England Republicans et cet.) were due to arrive. He breezed through the door, announced to the quivering [household] staff that the bar was on the wrong side of the room, had everyone in the place moving furniture, ashtrays, glasses. And he worked just as furiously and hard as anyone else. It did look better as he arranged it, too."

Ann was amused and perplexed by Rockefeller's indifference to his clothes.

"He was casual about them," she said. "Some of the clothes he wore were old-fashioned—he wore them for years. A friend of mine told me of going to his own tailor and finding the man busily making over a thirty-year-old tuxedo for Nelson. An overcoat Nelson wore was ragged across the collar. I joked with him about it. He finally got another one. You know you can influence a person by compliments as well as by criticism. I

complimented him when he came in wearing a blue shirt with a white collar."

Eisenhower was unbelievably dependent on his valet, Sergeant John Moaney, who had been his orderly in the army. Ambrose writes of the president, "He did not dress himself—John Moaney . . . put on his underwear, socks, shoes, pants, shirt, jacket, and tie. . . ." Eisenhower, it seems, seldom made his own decision on what to wear on any given day; he wore whatever suit Moaney laid out for him. On trips Moaney did the packing.

"The president could not have existed without Moaney," Ann said. "The governor had no valet. He packed for himself."

On June 11, 1973, Governor Rockefeller came to Ann's desk and asked her when her birthday was. "It's today, as a matter of fact," she answered. She was sixty-five. From his pocket he took an envelope and handed it to her. It contained two thousand shares of Eastern Airlines stock and a note expressing his gratitude for her "loyal friendship." The stock was then valued at $19,237. In the next six months the value declined. At Christmas that year, Rockefeller had another envelope for her, this one containing fourteen hundred shares of the International Basic Economy Corporation, valued at $3,545. This gift offset the decline in the Eastern Airlines shares.

Ann was among a score of Governor Rockefeller's senior assistants who received from him generous gifts, including money, in appreciation and reward for their work and loyalty. The money, which was in addition to their state salaries, was given in the form of loans that were not expected to be repaid. They ranged as high as $628,000 to William J. Ronan, a former secretary to the governor and later chairman of the board of the Port Authority of New York and New Jersey. Once dean of the School of Public Administration at New York University, Dr. Ronan had long been an adviser and mentor to Rockefeller. The governor lent Ann $25,000, ostensibly to meet some financial problems facing her after her retirement. At Christmas over the years, he gave her crystal, Japanese prints, engravings, and, in 1971, books from the library of his father, John D. Rockefeller, Jr., which she considered the most beautifully bound set she had ever seen. They were two volumes of *The Medici* by G. F. Young, with portraits and illustrations, published by E. P. Dutton in New York in 1923.

Rockefeller also gave Ann valuable jewelry. Among the pieces she particularly liked was a parrot pin. In January 1970, when she and Mary Stephens were in Puerto Rico, Ann's apartment on East Eighty-first Street in New York was robbed. The losses included the cherished twenty-dollar gold piece President Eisenhower had given her on her birthday in 1954. She wrote to Marie Clancy:

> All the nice jewelry Mrs. Levy gave me was gone, all the things I treasured from General Eisenhower. The Governor was really cute— he had given me two bracelets from Van Cleef & Arpels for Christmas and he claimed (I don't know whether he was telling the truth) that he had forgotten to have his floater policy taken off them. The first day I came back he presented me with another, and even more elegant bracelet.

On another occasion, Ann and Rockefeller were walking through the living room of his house on Foxhall Road in Washington, where he had a collection of Korean pottery that he himself had arranged in a cabinet. One piece in particular caught Ann's fancy. "I . . . made the awful error," she recalled, "of saying 'Oh, I'd love that!' " He opened the cabinet and gave it to her. "Others have had similar experiences," she said. "While at Foxhall Road . . . James Cannon remarked that he especially liked one of the chairs he saw there. [The governor] sent the chair to him. When Jim told [the governor] that he wanted to pay for the chair, [Rockefeller] refused to accept any payment, insisting that he sent the chair to Jim as a gift and that was that."

Years later the Internal Revenue Service brought an action against Ann, claiming that the stock she had received from Rockefeller in 1973 should have been declared as income. She challenged the action in court, maintaining that the stock, the jewelry, and other valuable items Rockefeller had presented her were gifts from an old friend and should be considered tax free. In an affidavit she said that for her to have refused them would have given him offense.

"To me," she added, "his gifts were simply manifestations of his generous nature and his affection and respect for me, and I always accepted them as such because I knew that is how he meant them. The value of any gift he ever made to me certainly was appropriate by his standards and in relation to his means. A gift of a $2,500 bracelet—or even $19,000 worth of stock—was no more to him, relatively, than any present I would give to a friend at Christmas or as a birthday present." Nelson Rockefeller's total fortune was about $218 million.

Ann won the case.

On December 11, 1973, nearly a year into his fourth term, Rockefeller resigned as governor of New York, the better, he judged, to position himself in the race for the Republican presidential nomination in 1976. He brought Ann back to New York with him on his own payroll, raising her salary from the nearly $37,000 a year she had received from the state to $40,000, soon increased to $42,500. Rockefeller's move came in the wake of advance tremors of what was to be one of the worst political earthquakes in American history. The tremors were generated by the forced resignation on October 10, 1973, of Vice-President Spiro T. Agnew for having accepted cash for alleged favors he had granted when he was governor of Maryland. To replace Agnew, President Nixon appointed Representative Gerald R. Ford of Michigan, Republican leader of the House of Representatives, as vice-president.

Rockefeller had scarcely settled down in New York as a private citizen at the start of 1974 when the political shocks grew worse as a result of the outpouring of disclosures in the Watergate scandal. On August 9, 1974, Nixon resigned rather than face impeachment. Ford moved into the White House, again leaving the vice-presidency vacant. While sitting in New

York wondering at this spectacle, Ann received a call from Seal Harbor. Rockefeller was on the line to confide to her that Ford wanted him as his vice-president.

Thus began a bizarre time in Ann's career, in large measure because Rockefeller was seized by the desire and belief that after two hundred years of our system of government, he was going to be, as she later described it, a "new kind of vice-president." Before accepting Ford's offer, he obtained assurance from the president that he, Rockefeller, would be a "working" vice-president. The kind of work he envisioned would have required broad executive power. When the time came for the appointment to be announced at the White House, Ann and some others on his staff joined Rockefeller at Stewart Air Force Base, near West Point, for a secret flight to Washington. After eight years there with Eisenhower, Ann had no doubt that she and the entire entourage were headed for the opposite end of the spectrum of the power, the prestige, and the exhilaration that Rockefeller coveted.

What she could not foresee was that she was headed into a conflict with Nelson Rockefeller that she would not long survive.

Once the news of his appointment was out, Rockefeller swept through Washington like a man whose dream had come true at last.

"He loved it at first," Ann recalled. "He went through a form of euphoria. I think he really thought he was going to be the next president."

His nomination was finally confirmed by Congress, and he was sworn in as vice-president on December 19, 1974, at the age of sixty-six. At Christmastime he gave a dinner party at Pocantico Hills for some of his staff and friends. When he entered, Ann was on his arm. He announced that he had appointed her chief of staff to the vice-president.

Her first task of reopening the vice-presidential office in the Executive Office Building in the next block of Pennsylvania Avenue west of the White House was a busy one. Ford had suddenly vacated it in August. Since Rockefeller's nomination as vice-president, thousands of letters had arrived for him, but because four months had elapsed before his confirmation, no one had been on hand to open them. Ann had to borrow people from Albany to systematize the handling of accumulated mail. She had to decide how many secretaries were needed, had to hire them (she assigned four to herself), and had to set their salaries. Space had to be found for James Cannon, Richard Dunham, Hugh Morrow, Joseph Persico, and Harry Albright, all of whom Rockefeller was bringing to Washington with him. Among her own assistants, Ann brought down Kathy Huldrum and Nancy Towel, colleagues in the New York office, and gave them some personal advice: enjoy Washington. Ann told them not to do as she had done during the Eisenhower administration, namely, work all the time, often to the exclusion of social life. When the State Department asked the vice-president's office for a list of names of female employees who might be considered as guests at diplomatic social functions, Ann insisted that Nancy and Kathy sign up.

One of Ann's appointments was not routine. Rockefeller asked her to give a job to Susan J. Herter, who had been a friend of his at least since she had worked for him in the State Department in the 1940s. Considerably younger than Ann, Mrs. Herter was then the daughter-in-law of former Secretary of State Herter. Ann assigned her, with a secretary of her own, to one of the offices adjoining Rockefeller's and wanted her to take charge of correspondence. Mrs. Herter, a capable and experienced woman, did not want that job. Ann said later she never was certain what Mrs. Herter did. Ann was convinced that the job Mrs. Herter wanted was her own, chief of staff. Her salary was $30,000 a year, compared with Ann's $42,500. Members of the staff considered Susan Herter to be an aggressive woman. It was accepted around the office that the two women did not get along well together. "Oil and water," Dunham said afterward. No doubt an element of their incompatibility was that each woman had her own claim on Rockefeller's friendship.

Rockefeller meanwhile was soaring in his own orbit. All that he heard from Ford filled him with optimism. The first thing the president said publicly after Rockefeller was sworn in was that the new vice-president would be "a good partner for me." Then the White House announced that Rockefeller would be vice-chairman of the Domestic Council, a body created in the Nixon administration to make the ultimate recommendations to the president in domestic affairs, as the National Security Council does on military and diplomatic strategy.

"Ford and Rockefeller stimulated each other," Dunham recalled.

"Rockefeller intellectually understood the infirmities of the vice-presidency," Albright said afterward. "But Ford was expansive about the role Rockefeller could play, and Rockefeller inhaled. He really knew better, but he really inhaled."

Rockefeller was not a man who appreciated nay-saying. "The governor didn't like to be discouraged or have anyone challenge what was his ability and preference," recalled T. Norman Hurd, a former New York State budget director. "He was determined things were going to work to suit him." Rockefeller especially did not like nay-saying when he was, to use Albright's expression, "inhaling." Nevertheless, on one of their first flights together from New York to Washington after he was confirmed, Rockefeller said to Ann that he wanted to benefit from her unusual experience in the White House. "If you ever see or hear of me doing the wrong thing, tell me," he asserted, as she recalled his words. Long afterward she remarked to Persico, "Then he proceeded to do everything wrong. And he got annoyed if I pointed it out." Ann was particularly distressed that Rockefeller believed he had been given carte blanche by the president.

From his talks with Ford, Rockefeller was convinced that the president wanted him to have the authority to do in the domestic field that which Secretary of State Kissinger did in the international area. When, early in 1975, however, Rockefeller sought to have this authority confirmed in an executive order, he collided with the White House staff, particularly Donald H. Rumsfeld, formerly of Nixon's staff and now staff coordinator and assistant to President Ford. According to Robert T. Hartmann, chief speechwriter and counselor to Ford, Rumsfeld was worried "about Ford being eclipsed, or his staff being bypassed, by a strong-willed vice-president." Rockefeller asked that whoever was named executive director of the Domestic Council report to Ford through the vice-president. A tough-minded former member of the House of Representatives from Illinois, Rumsfeld balked. He interpreted Rockefeller's proposal as one that would in effect make Rockefeller acting president for domestic policy, causing Ford virtually to abdicate his authority in that field. Furthermore, Rumsfeld already had his own candidate for executive director of the Domestic Council, Professor Phillip Areeda of Harvard.

Upon learning of Rumsfeld's opposition, Rockefeller confronted him angrily. Rumsfeld's opposition was only strengthened by his suspicion that Rockefeller was also trying to cut *him* out of a share of responsibility for domestic policy. Rebuffed, Rockefeller returned to his own office intent on dictating a note of protest to Ford. Ann discouraged him from doing it.

"She knew Nelson Rockefeller couldn't run over people in the White House," Cannon recalled. Nevertheless, Cannon faulted Rumsfeld for trying to pick a fight with the vice-president.

Ann's admonition to Rockefeller pigeonholed the idea of a letter of protest to the president. On reflection, Rockefeller concluded that the executive director of the Domestic Council need not report to the president through the vice-president. Instead, Rockefeller decided, it would be satisfactory for his purposes if the president appointed Rockefeller's own men as the top staff executives of the council. He informed Ann that he would propose Jim Cannon for executive director and Dunham as deputy director.

"You've got the wrong man," Ann said, in regard to Cannon. The wiser choice, she argued, would be to make Dunham, a former New York State budget director, the executive director of the council because the council's work involved subjects like funding and program analysis. Cannon was an extremely competent and appealing man in the political, legislative, and public relations fields but, unlike Dunham, was not an expert in budgets and program analysis.

"They will chew Jim up," Ann told Rockefeller. The term was not accurate, but the point was. Placing Cannon in the executive director's post—and Dunham in the deputy director's spot, too, for that matter—would enmesh them in the very White House staff that Rockefeller was battling and would saddle them with divided loyalties between the president and the vice-president. If Rockefeller was vice-chairman of the Domestic Council, Ford was chairman ex officio.

Although Rockefeller did not dispute Ann's point, he countered by saying that with Cannon as executive director, he, Rockefeller, could then control the council himself.

"That is not the way it is done in the White House," Ann replied.

Neither was Ann's forthrightness the manner in which members of his staff customarily tried to dissuade Rockefeller from doing something. Indirection was the general rule. Robert Douglass, formerly special counsel to Governor Rockefeller, once explained the accepted technique to Dunham. He said: "Dick, when he asks you to do something improbable, don't tell him the obstacles. Tell him yes, right away. Of course, it can be done. Then casually mention a few problems."

Harry Albright, who, on one occasion in the Domestic Council controversy, had heard Ann tell Rockefeller, "Governor, that won't work; it will never work," said later that Ann was one of the few persons who said straight out to Rockefeller, "You can't do this."

Rockefeller was greatly encouraged by a speech President Ford made at the Waldorf-Astoria in New York on February 13, 1975, at a Republican fund-raising dinner in honor of the new vice-president. Ford announced not only that he had asked the vice-president "to personally and vigorously oversee" the work of the Domestic Council but also that he was appointing Cannon and Dunham to the two top staff jobs. Areeda's name passed out of the picture. Three other Rockefeller assistants also were to work under Cannon and Dunham. To some in the enthusiastic gathering that night it seemed that the historic role of the vice-president was being recast.

Back in Washington, Rockefeller's vision of the expanding power of the vice-president troubled Ann. Years afterward she was convinced that he had gone through some kind of deterioration, affecting his judgment, a deterioration that continued, she thought, until his death in New York on January 27, 1979. He would return to the vice-president's office from a meeting with Ford and tell her excitedly that he was going to "run" the White House. She was disgusted. And when Ann Whitman was disgusted, Nelson Rockefeller was not likely to have missed it.

The friction with the White House staff made it disagreeable for Ann to carry out one of her duties, which was to attend, often with Cannon, the daily 8 A.M. White House senior staff conference. As a member of the vice-president's staff, entering such a meeting, chaired by Rumsfeld or his deputy, Richard B. Cheney, was an altogether different experience for Ann from stepping into a Sherman Adams staff conference as confidential secretary to the president.

"I hated to go," she said of the 1975 meetings, "because I didn't feel I was accepted by the White House staff, although some, like General Scowcroft and Jack Marsh, were terribly nice to me.* It means a lot to me whether I am accepted. Try being a woman in a group like that! I was a representative of the vice-president. He was not popular with that group. They thought he was trying to take control. He *was* trying to take control. In no sense did I feel equal. I was not comfortable. Governor Adams's staff conferences were much more informal. There I went in as an equal. They were much more pleasant and fun to go to."

After each staff conference, Ann would report to Rockefeller any information or impressions she thought he needed to have.

The arrangements regarding the Domestic Council were

---

* Air Force Lieutenant General Brent Scowcroft was then deputy assistant to the president for national security affairs; John O. Marsh, Jr., was counselor to the president.

not working out to his satisfaction. In his new role, for example, Cannon had the title of assistant to the president for domestic affairs. He was on the White House payroll. His office was in the White House. The same was true of Dunham. Their primary loyalty, therefore, was necessarily to the president, not the vice-president. In certain differences between the White House and the vice-president's office over the functions of the Domestic Council, this fact became apparent, though obviously it was not accepted by Rockefeller. Working under the president, with the paperwork handled in the White House, Cannon did not have the latitude to do what Rockefeller sometimes wanted him to do. Hence Cannon, as Persico records, "felt the killing frost of Rockefeller's disfavor."

Once Rockefeller returned from a meeting with Ford manifesting what Ann described as an air of "I can do anything if I want to." He talked about becoming chief of staff in the White House. Ann was incredulous and annoyed. How could a vice-president be chief of staff to a president? Rockefeller's meaning did not become clear for years. At a conference sponsored by the University of California at San Diego in January 1986, Richard Cheney described what he called the "major problem" of Ford's staff in handling relations with the vice-president. According to Cheney, every Wednesday afternoon at Ford and Rockefeller's regular weekly meeting, Rockefeller would enter the Oval Office and hand Ford a new domestic policy proposal. Every Wednesday night, Cheney said, Ford would meet with his senior staff and say, "What the hell do I do with this?" Nevertheless, each proposal was "staffed out," related Cheney. And every time the conclusion was that implementation of the Rockefeller proposal would be inconsistent with Ford's prevailing policy. With the punishing climb of inflation since the Vietnam War and with Governor Ronald Reagan of California threatening to challenge Ford for the 1976 Republican nomination (as he did, unsuccessfully), Ford moved toward a moratorium on most new domestic programs.

In the midst of all this, Cheney said that he and Rockefeller reached a state of "total hostility." Rockefeller thereupon told

Ford that the only way he would serve in a second Ford administration was as White House chief of staff and not as vice-president. Obviously this was the background of Rockefeller's statement to Ann about becoming chief of staff. It is not likely that he found her reaction comforting. Times had turned sour for him.

EPILOGUE

In June 1975, six months after Rockefeller became vice-president, Ann was back in New York, handling his personal affairs. Her salary remained $42,500. Her career in public life, which had begun in the 1952 presidential campaign, was over. The shift to New York had been a sudden one. Rockefeller decided to make a change. Susan Herter was appointed chief of staff. The event embittered Ann then, and her feelings remained sore for a long time. She stayed in the new job for two years, then retired in June 1977. In those final twenty-four months her relations with Rockefeller were good. To the end of his life, he retained a deep affection for her, a respect for her abilities, and gratitude for what she had done for him. Why he suddenly changed chiefs of staff in the vice-presidential office he never said, and no one else can. What comes immediately to mind in the circumstances is Persico's remark about Cannon's having felt "the killing frost of Rockefeller's disfavor." It was an axiom among his associates that Rockefeller soon tired of being told he could not do what he wanted to do. That such advice may have been the soul of sagacity was beside the point.

While, as Ann said, he may have been ahead of his time in the advancement of women, in at least a couple of cases before hers he had lavished his attention and favor on a bright woman, promoted her, and then, inexplicably, walked past her desk without looking at her. After a long period of such indifference, painful and bewildering for the woman, he would appoint her to a lucrative post, perhaps on a quasi-judicial body, if she had the qualifications, and one that she might be able to hold for years.

Of course, it is possible that Ann displeased Rockefeller in some unstated way besides telling him when his actions were unwise. It is even conceivable that, after experiencing her disenchantment and dismay over his difficulties in the vice-presidency, he simply believed she would be happier to return to New York and escape a depressing scene.

Things only got worse for him after she left. Far from controlling domestic policy, Rockefeller was not even informed in advance of an important tax program Ford had decided to submit to Congress. Then, in the fall of 1975, Ford yielded to conservative voices in the party and agreed to seek a new running mate in 1976, dropping Rockefeller for, as it turned out, Senator Robert J. Dole of Kansas. Bored, Rockefeller made the vice-presidency a Monday-to-Friday job, spending weekends at Pocantico Hills with Happy and their two sons, who had never moved to Washington, ostensibly to avoid interrupting the boys' schooling. Friends also believed that Happy was not eager to be involved in the day-to-day political life of Washington. The early bustle was gone from the vice-president's office. Cannon was in the White House. Dunham had been appointed by the president as chairman of the Federal Power Commission. Albright, who had not planned to stay in Washington for more than a few months, was back in the banking business in New York. Leaving when she did did not detract from Ann's remarkable career. Moreover, she was then already two years beyond what was the generally accepted retirement age of sixty-five. More than a decade after stopping work in 1977, she still reads three or four serious books a week. Her health, which saw her through the strenuous years in politics and government, remains good. She is still friendly, quick-witted, risible, and curious about events. She is well aware that historians are reading her papers in the Dwight D. Eisenhower Library in Abilene, Kansas, and citing her as an authority in their books. When in New York in the warm months, she frequently lunches with old friends, some of them going back to the days with Adele Levy, who died on March 12, 1960. In winter months in Clearwater, she regularly sees her devoted friends, Tom and Mary Stephens, who live in an apartment near hers.

During the school's brief existence she was a member of the board of trustees of Eisenhower College at Schenectady, New York, and she remains a trustee of the Eisenhower Institute of World Affairs. Among its other activities, it is the organization in charge of the planning for an elaborate international Eisenhower Centennial in 1990.

Still, retirement has not been easy for Ann. It has often meant loneliness and is empty of the scenes and excitement that she relished about "life at the top." The wound of divorce from Whit never fully healed, and Ed Allen's strokes distressed her and deprived her of the enjoyment of his companionship. He died on September 18, 1986. Whit died in 1987. Sometimes on winter days in her apartment on Sand Key, in Clearwater, on the Gulf of Mexico, Ann likes to sit on her seventh-floor terrace and gaze, as she said whimsically, "on the blue-green water with the white sails racing away in the distance." She would hardly make a point of it, but she is proud of having spent more than twenty years as the confidential secretary and assistant to two of the leading American public figures of the second half of the twentieth century. She remained fond of Rockefeller during the forty years of their friendship until his death. But Dwight D. Eisenhower was the towering figure in her life. Two weeks after he had left office, she sent him a note. It read:

February 4, 1961

Dear Mr. President:

I can't say it. But thank you for eight and a half years—years when I had the opportunity to learn (and I did learn, a little), the opportunity to meet people and go places (which I loved), and the opportunity to have quiet moments with the greatest and most wonderful man on earth (and perhaps I absorbed a tiny bit of wisdom). I shall think of you every hour and every day and wish I could be with you.

and please tear this up!

a.

NOTES ON SOURCES

The material in this book comes from several basic sources. One is the author's remembered observations as a reporter who covered the Eisenhower White House and who has known Mrs. Whitman for nearly forty years. Another is the Ann C. Whitman Diary Series in the Eisenhower Library in Abilene. A third source are books that have been written on Eisenhower and Rockefeller. A good deal of the material in this book comes from the many interviews the author has had with Mrs. Whitman since 1985 and from his other interviews with her longtime friends and former colleagues. Much material, too, comes from her personal letters and notes to Edmund Whitman, to Mrs. Levy, and to other friends. The author also had access to some other miscellaneous notes Mrs. Whitman made and to several pages of an autobiographical manuscript she began years ago and then abandoned. She also wrote the author letters answering questions he had put to her in writing. None of these letters, notes, abstracts of interviews, or similar material mentioned above are deposited in a collection in any library or archive. Where pertinent, sources are herein indicated, chapter by chapter.

□ 1 □

"Mamie and Ike will recognize all the values you have and are," taken from a letter, Edward Bernays to Ann C. Whitman (ACW), June 6, 1952, now in ACW's personal papers. Her description of the scenes and preconvention activities in Denver are drawn from ACW's letters to Adele Levy, Edmund Whitman, and to the author (RJD). Also from interviews with Abbott and Wanda Allender Washburn. "Quite a temperamental lady" is quoted in Stephen E. Ambrose, *Eisenhower: Volume Two. The President* (New York, 1984), p. 644. On Franklin D. Roosevelt and Stanley High, see *FDR: An Intimate History* (Garden City, NY, 1983), p. 383. "A passion for the excitement of life at the top" is quoted from a letter, ACW to RJD, April 18, 1985.

□ 2 □

"That Eisenhower could not have gotten through his task without her goes without saying" is from Ambrose's *Eisenhower*, p. 676.

□ 3 □

Facts about Rosenwald are drawn from M. R. Werner, *Julius Rosenwald: The Life of a Practical Humanitarian* (New York, 1939), pp. 34, 38ff. This chapter also relies on interviews with ACW, Trude Lash, Marion Rosenwald Ascoli, and Abbott and Wanda Allender Washburn. C.D. Jackson's remark to William J. Miller is recalled in a letter from Miller to RJD, November 8, 1985.

4

Eisenhower described ACW as his confidential secretary and assistant in the inscription on a photograph, which he gave her at the end of his term. A "repository of insider background" comes from RJD's interview with Joseph E. Persico, author of a memoir of life on Governor Rockefeller's staff. Hagerty quotes on ACW are from an unpublished story that Charles Roberts filed to *Newsweek* from Washington on March 26, 1958, copy supplied to RJD by Roberts. Sherman Adams's comments on ACW were contained in a letter, Adams to RJD, April 17, 1985. "Ragtime Cowboy Joe": music by Lewis F. Muir and Maurice Abrahams, words by Grant Clarke. For Eisenhower on his son's death see Dwight D. Eisenhower, *At Ease: Stories I Tell to Friends* (Garden City, NY, 1967), pp. 108–82. The account of Archbishop Athenagoras's visit is told in Thomas E. Stephens, *Columbia University Oral History Project*, January 12, 1968, p. 49. "The lack of response . . . astonished and infuriated me" is in a letter, ACW to RJD, May 6, 1985.

5

Interviews with Bryce N. Harlow, William F. Hopkins, Andrew J. Goodpaster, and Roemer McPhee. For H. R. Haldeman and "the Ann Whitman end run" see William H. Safire, "Two Women in an Archway," *The New York Times*, August 22, 1974, p. 33. "What in the hell are prayerful good wishes?" is taken from RJD interview with Mary Caffrey Stephens.

The president's two letters to Admiral Joy are in the central files of the Eisenhower Library. The story of the encounter with the gardner at the Soviet Embassy is from Stephens's oral history, *Columbia University Oral History Project*, pp. 21, 22.

A copy of the letter to James C. Stahlman is in ACW's personal papers. Her diary entries concerning her experiences at the time of Eisenhower's heart attack have been included in Robert H. Ferrell, ed., *The Eisenhower Diaries* (New York, 1981), p. 302ff. Russell Baker's story was in *The New York Times*, September 26, 1955, p. 15.

□ 8 □

Freeman Gosden is quoted in Jacqueline Cochran's oral history transcript, interview no. 2, p. 206, in the Eisenhower Library. Wilton B. Persons's comments on Eisenhower's trip to Panama are quoted in Ambrose's *Eisenhower*, p. 335.

□ 9 □

Eisenhower's correspondence with Everett E. (Swede) Hazlett has been collected in Robert Griffith, ed., *Ike's Letter to a Friend* (Lawrence, Kansas, 1984).

□ 10 □

For Adams's account of his "imprudent" conduct see Sherman Adams, *First-Hand Report: The Story of the Eisenhower Administration* (New York, 1961), chap. 21.

□ 11 □

ACW's account of her first jet flight to Europe is in her diary, dated Aug. 26–Sept. 7, 1959. Kevin McCann's quote upon returning from the India Trip is in Merriam Smith, *A President's Odyssey* (New York, 1961), p. 85.

□ 12 □

Interview with Alice Boyce. ACW's account of her last morning in the White House, January 20, 1961, is from her unfinished manuscript.

Eisenhower's remarks on Rockefeller's halting moves toward becoming a presidential candidate are in Ambrose's *Eisenhower*, p. 595. "She ran the White House for Ike" is taken from an RJD interview with Hugh Morrow, a Rockefeller speechwriter and spokesman. The long passage on ACW comments about Rockefeller and Eisenhower, their similarities and dissimilarities, is a composite, carefully kept in context, of observations obtained from her in interviews with RJD. The chapter also includes material drawn from other interviews with Joseph W. Canzeri, James M. Cannon, Nancy Towel, Joseph Persico, Mary McAniff Kresky, Richard L. Dunham, Harry Albright, and T. Norman Hurd.

"It will cost you" is taken from an interview with Oscar Reubhausen, a Rockefeller adviser. "It may be a bit drastic" is quoted in Joseph E. Persico, *The Imperial Rockefeller: A Biography of Nelson A. Rockefeller*, (New York, 1982), p. 144, which also cites (on p. 267) Rockefeller's belief that he would be a "working" vice-president, as well as ACW's quote "Then he proceeded to do everything wrong" (p. 285). The two paragraphs beginning "It was Rockefeller's conviction" and ending "Ann discouraged him from doing it" draw upon Robert T. Hartmann, *Palace Politics: An Inside Account of the Ford Years* (New York, 1980), pp. 288, 304, 306, and 307–308. Robert Douglass's advice to Dunham is noted in Persico, *The Imperial Rockefeller*, p. 178, as is Cannon's feeling "the killing frost of Rockefeller's disfavor" (p. 286). For a report on the conference in San Diego see David Broder, "Ex-Aides Swap Tips on Serving the Boss in the White House," *Washington Post*, January 19, 1986, p. A5.

□ Epilogue □

A copy of ACW's note of February 4, 1961, is in her personal papers.

INDEX